I Hear You Talking, Job

I Hear You Talking, Job

by
Wilford V. Prindle

Beacon Hill Press of Kansas City
Kansas City, Missouri

To my wife,
Doris,
who helped me most to live it;
and to my friend
Ollin Wineland,
who encouraged me most to write it.

Oh, that my words were recorded,
that they were written on a scroll,
that they were inscribed with an
iron tool on lead,
or engraved in rock forever!
I know that my Redeemer lives,
and that in the end he will stand
upon the earth.
And after my skin has been destroyed,
yet in my flesh I will see God.

                         Job 19:23-26, NIV

Contents

Preface		11
1 / To Quit or Not to Quit		13
2 / To Comfort, Confuse, or Condemn		20
3 / From Birth Through Rebirth		34
4 / From Rebirth to Retirement		43
5 / God Cares for His Own		58
6 / Reasons and Responses		68
7 / The Struggle with Responsibility		75
8 / God Took His Own Medicine		86
9 / Though He Slay Me		92

Preface

It was never my intention to write an autobiography. Such a goal would necessarily have resulted in a much larger book. In order, however, to explore the causes and evidence of my illness and relate that illness to my activities, it has been necessary to present certain segments of my life.

The scattered pattern of a discharged shotgun shell illustrates the multiplicity of purposes far better than the single hole made by a rifle bullet. Frustration, not inspiration, brought about the initiation of this project. I became wearied with questions such as, "Why would a Christian worker be disabled?" or "Why wouldn't God heal His ministers?" or "Why would a minister suffer such excruciating pain?" The "whys" seemed to bother others more than me. It seemed necessary to deal with divine healing even though this treatment may seem inept to some.

Once begun, inspiration seemed to take charge. A better understanding of the extent of Jesus' sufferings made me realize that although the Lord might not elect to heal in this life, He cares and suffers with us. I became concerned that those who suffer without Jesus might come to realize they could endure suffering better with a personal Savior.

Osteoporosis has only recently begun to receive the publicity it should have. This victim desires to warn all ages, especially the young, of the terrible consequences of a calcium-deficient diet.

Finally, it would be a very useful service if our churches would have periodic studies on how to visit the sick. These studies should relate to all illnesses, suffering, and disability. You will discover other worthwhile goals as you read the book.

No doubt this would be a better work if I were free from pain and physical problems. As it is, I first wrote every word in longhand while lying in bed. When able, I typed the manuscript, often in 30-minute to 45-minute periods. Much depended upon the availability of medication and, sometimes, even the weather. Some days it was necessary to omit all typing periods. Nevertheless, I have found the preparation of this work to be a blessing. It has given me a better understanding of this affliction, a sense of accomplishment, and a deeper joy in the Lord.

To Quit or Not to Quit

Thank You, dear Jesus, for that service; and thank You that it's over," I breathed while pushing my body back firmly into the orthopedic car seat that was on the passenger side of our car. We had just completed an all-day homecoming and mortgage-burning service. Although I had taken an excessive amount of pain medication, my lower back was hurting severely. Doris, my wife, separated herself from the friendly people as rapidly as she could. She was to drive to a hospital where I would check in by 4 P.M. for major surgery scheduled at seven o'clock the next morning.

As we drove out of the church parking lot, my wife glanced at me. I was mopping cold perspiration from my face that, no doubt, registered a considerable amount of pain. "You just must give it up," she said.

"Give up what?" I asked in a disgruntled tone, as if unaware of what she meant. We had discussed the subject a number of times. It was amazing how depressed one could feel so soon after such a victorious service as we had just experienced.

"The pastorate," she replied patiently. "You know you're killing yourself with all that pain medication. Besides, the stress from not accomplishing all you expect of yourself certainly doesn't help."

She was correct about the state of my health and about the complications brought on by stress, but I had always felt one did not just give up the ministry. My public surrender to the call of God to preach the gospel was more soul-shaking to me than any other experience, even being born again. At the time I was a buyer for Sears, Roebuck and Company in the Mail Order Division. It meant giving up a job I liked and had worked hard to get. It meant forsaking Sears' profit-sharing plan, clearly the best in the country at that time. It meant abandoning our plans for a new house, something we had dreamed of for years. My wife did not work outside the home because we had three small children. We knew the ministry would bring us face-to-face with uncertain financial circumstances. This was not eased by the conviction, already strongly felt before I made the call public, that we should make plans for college and seminary work during the earliest possible years of ministry.

I accepted Christ at age 28, and my life immediately became a whirlwind of activity. Within the first month I began teaching a Sunday School class of young adults. During the next month I was elected president of our men's group. The next year I became Sunday School superintendent. I found there was nothing I liked better than to visit, especially the lost. I would teach, worship, and visit all day on Sunday and suffer a terrible letdown on Monday. Very early in my Christian life I wished that I could do Christian work all the time.

Soon after becoming Sunday School superintendent,

I was "set aside" to be ordained a deacon. This did not happen, however, because I surrendered to preach, accepted the call of my first pastorate, and was ordained a minister instead. Doris, who had accepted Christ in the same service as I, was just as involved as I in the life of the church. Nevertheless, I dreaded telling her about my call to the ministry. When I did, she simply said, "I have been wondering when you were going to answer it." She probably knew at least as soon as I. The Lord blessed my early ministry far beyond my expectations and, no doubt, those of many others.

These experiences were very encouraging and supportive in the years ahead when I was so ill it seemed really impossible to continue. It was our privilege to serve five pastorates over approximately 30 years, in four states, without missing a Sunday between churches. We never felt called away from any of our congregations but, rather, called to new pastoral challenges. I have mentioned my love for certain areas of Christian work. I lived to preach. Can you not understand why the word "quit," when applied to the pastorate, was difficult to even consider?

At the time of this trip to the hospital, and our conversation about quitting, I had suffered severely and continually for 12 years from a serious back injury. There had been times when the idea of continuing was almost too much. Because the Lord had always given His grace, and His people had been so understanding and helpful, I managed to persevere. I still loved the work of the ministry, even in pain, and most of the time I was confident that God, in some manner, would soon heal.

"Just how do you propose we eat if I quit?" I asked Doris. That was a reprehensible question in the light of the Lord's constant provision for us during all the years we had known Him. We had been Christians about three months when the Sunday School lesson was on tithing. I went to the pastor and told him I had to give up the class. I could not teach some-

15

thing I did not and could not do because we had too many "easy" payments to make. He persuaded me to try tithing the next Sunday, just one Sunday, and to teach the class at least one more time. Maybe he believed that if I once taught tithing, I would do it. If so, he was right.

The next week, the day before payday, my merchandise manager walked casually into my office. "By the way," he said, "you've got a raise."

"A raise? I didn't think it was time for that yet."

"It isn't," he replied. "I guess somebody upstairs likes you."

He was referring to either the merchandise superintendent or the general plant manager, but my thoughts went higher. I could think only of the Lord.

"Oh yes," he said as he left, "that's retroactive for a couple of weeks. It will be on tomorrow's check."

It was hard to believe. The raise was enough to take care of our tithe. Even when I had asked to be relieved from teaching because of the lesson on the tithe, the Lord had already made provision for me to be able to do it without any hardship. I discreetly asked around and found I was the only buyer who received a raise. It may have been just a salary adjustment to my job status; but as long as I'm on this earth, I'll believe it came from the Lord.

When I left Sears to begin college, the final check had two weeks of unexpected salary. I tried to convince Accounting they had made a mistake. They insisted that, since my resignation was effective after the first of the year, I had two weeks vacation pay due. My anniversary was November 11, and the resignation was effective January 20. It seemed a short time to earn two weeks of vacation. Finally I accepted it, and we gave thanks to God for the unexpected windfall.

When buyers departed in the good graces of the company, and that was usually only at retirement, they were given a party by the salaried employees. It was decided the usual type of party was not compatible with my entering the ministry. One of the other buyers, a very rare "visible" Christian, was commissioned to spend the money on me instead of a party. This Christian friend purchased a copy of Strong's *Exhaustive Concordance of the Bible,* a set of commentaries, and a desk set composed of two Parker pens, a marble slab, and a plate engraved with my name and a suitable inscription. These did me far more good than a farewell cocktail party. The concordance still gets quite frequent use. It seemed, even in this incident, the Lord was taking care of my needs.

We used the profit-sharing money to pay the mortgage on our small home and buy a bargain-priced 1948 Kaiser-Fraser car. It gave us the feel of a luxury car without the usual luxury price. One day that spring when we had begun to scrape the bottom of the barrel, a letter came from Sears that looked like a bill. Oh, no! I thought. Please don't let it be something I've neglected to pay. The windowed envelope contained a letter and a check. The general plant manager had written that although I was no longer with the company, the consensus was that I should share in the annual bonus of the department. My share was nearly $700. The check was for one-half that amount; the other half had been deducted for income tax. Of course the latter was refunded the following year just when we needed it most. Seven hundred dollars may not seem like much in these inflated times, but it looked like a fortune to us in 1950.

The salary from my first pastorate (really two churches pastored simultaneously) was not large, but we've never eaten better. Every meal on the church fields was like a Thanksgiving dinner. We often arrived at one church on Friday evening so that I would have more time to make calls. The people always had made provision for us far enough in advance to give us direction as to where to go when we reached the area. Every Sunday night we would take home a car trunk full of food. Many in our congregations were farmers. It seemed we almost always had fresh meat, eggs, butter, fresh vegetables and fruit in season, and all kinds of canned food. When I accepted a church in the Independence, Mo., area, the salary was raised $10.00 per week between the time of accepting their call and the actual assumption of the pastorate. We never had to worry about food or finances even when I was unable to work. Yes indeed, asking how we would eat if I quit was a question that reflected adversely on my faith. The Lord had always provided. Why would He stop if we were doing the best we could?

Of course, I did not recall all of these incidents on the short drive to the hospital, but I was aware of how the Lord had cared for us. Doris ignored my seeming ungratefulness and replied to my question, "We'll investigate disability, and I'll find some kind of work if necessary."

"Sure you will," I remarked sarcastically. "Employers are falling all over each other to hire females in their 50s without job skills; and, as far as disability is concerned, they're not about to give anything to a preacher as long as he can open his mouth and speak."

I began to sense some irritation when my wife said, "Why won't you realize everything doesn't depend on what you do? You have great faith in the Lord's provision as long as you're well and strong, but you lose it at the thought of your not being able to work. Remember how often you've said you didn't have to put up with something, and you could make a living digging ditches if you had to? Well, you can't dig ditches now. You're going to have to really depend on faith. You know the Lord won't let us starve."

"But there is still much to be done: things I know how to do, and things I need to do," I responded somewhat lamely.

"Maybe you should remember Dr. Shepard now." Doris smiled as she said it.

I knew instantly what she meant. Dr. W. L. Muncy, Jr.,

had told us the story in his missions class. It seems there was a certain Dr. Shepard who pastored a rather large church and felt he could not spare the time for a vacation. Church members urged him to take some time off, and his wife and doctor virtually insisted upon it. Troubled in his own mind, one night he dreamed he went to heaven to talk it over with the Lord. He was escorted through enormous double doors into a gigantic room. There was a thick carpet runner down the center of it, and at the far end was a mammoth desk. The Lord was sitting behind the desk. He was weeping with His head cradled in His arms. "Dear Lord, what is the matter?" anxiously ventured Dr. Shepard. The Lord answered without raising His head, "Oh, Dr. Shepard plans to take a two weeks vacation, and I don't know what on earth I will do without him on the job."

Feeling chagrined as I thought of the rebuke in the story, I said, "Let me pray and think about it while I'm in the hospital, and we'll try to make a decision when I return home."

After checking into the hospital, I quickly fell into the routine of being prepared for early morning surgery. One often wonders if this flurry of activity is not partly designed to keep the patient's mind off what may seem a frightening experience. I spent what little time I could, thinking about my future, or the lack of it, as a pastor. In fact, I went to sleep praying about it that night. How could I ask God to allow me to quit while the church was still making progress? Actually it appeared to be in a position to make a great forward thrust. The question was, "Could I lead it in such a program?" To quit, or not to quit, really was the decision to be made, and it was exceedingly difficult for this pastor.

2

To Comfort, Confuse, or Condemn

Spending a few days in a hospital bed certainly wasn't a new experience. In general, hospitals have similar routines. If one is fortunate enough to have good friends, a number of visitors will find their way into your daily schedule. This may be good or bad, depending on the circumstances.

The main purpose of this chapter is to call attention to a few of the many ways Christendom deals with suffering and disability. The Indian often accused the white man of having a forked tongue. Christians speak with many tongues on these subjects. During an extended tour of America, Dr. Helmut Thielicke, esteemed European theologian, was asked what he considered the greatest fault of American Christians might be. "They have an inadequate view of suffering," he replied. It is doubtful that most of us have studied and prayed enough about sickness to really know what we believe.

I don't pretend to understand the inequitable distribution of suffering, as I have witnessed it around the world, but I can speak with some degree of authority from personal experience as both a patient and a visitor of the sick. After 10 major surgeries and several minor ones, 18 hospitalizations, 12 years of serving as a semi-invalid pastor and finally total disability, I feel I am acquainted with the attitudes of many Christian people who call on the sick. Viewing the subject from the "other side of the blanket," I have spent nearly 40 years calling on those who were ill, often accompanied by another minister or layperson. This has afforded good opportunities to study the reactions of the ailing to the words and attitudes of their visitors.

Please understand that this is not intended to discourage visitation of the sick. The right kind of visit can introduce a bit of heaven into a patient's difficult day and, possibly, produce better results than medication. It is certainly worth the effort needed to prepare ourselves to be better visitors. The half-dozen examples that follow are, admittedly, negative in nature. They aren't as ridiculous as the visitor who stood on the patient's oxygen tube, or the one who stumbled over and broke the circuit of his life-support system. This is an effort to reveal the fact that careless remarks and the employment of doubtful theology may sometimes be more disturbing and painful to patients than their physical afflictions.

The Cross You Bear

The statement we hear most often is, "This is just the cross given you to bear." It is usually delivered with sympathy, resignation, and a sober wisdom. I can't accept this statement as truth unless, in some way, this suffering will bring others to Christ, and even then, not always. Jesus told would-be followers to take up their individual crosses, but He always added that they were to follow Him. Jesus' cross meant a life sacrificed to save sinners. Our Christian crosses

21

must mean the same! Furthermore, like Jesus we must accept them voluntarily! Consider a person who yields to the call to a church-related vocation and follows the leadership of the Lord, regardless of the consequences. That person is bearing his cross! My illness tends toward the prevention of following Him as I wish. As a rule, we can reach more people for Christ with healthy bodies than with those shackled to beds of illness most of the time. We would not volunteer for a life of illness if we had a choice. However, those who view suffering and disability in the category of a cross to bear are often among the most spiritual.

Perhaps an event from my life will indicate the fine line between bearing one's cross and simply responding to an opportunity. Probably most of our Independence, Mo., congregation believed the Lord arranged my hospital experiences, as a patient, because He wanted some particular person won. I sometimes wondered about it also. It is true I was given the blessing of winning at least one during each hospitalization. Bear with me now for one such incident that could make unmistakable what is meant by bearing one's cross.

Once I was sent to the Veterans Hospital in Wadsworth, Kans., because the Kansas City hospital was full. As an ambulatory patient hospitalized for some tests and surgery, I was placed in a ward of 16 patients where all but one could walk. After walking back to the ward from breakfast on the second day, I began a conversation with a fellow patient. I told him I was a preacher, and we changed the topic of our talk to the Bible. As other patients returned, some joined us. Soon we moved some chairs over to where the main aisle in the ward intersected the hallway aisle coming into the ward. It became routine to have a Bible discussion after breakfast each morning before our other activities began. Men came from some of the other rooms and wards on the floor. We continued this informal meeting for over two weeks until I had surgery.

I became concerned about the one man in our ward who was not ambulatory because he seemed to watch and listen so intently to our group. One evening all the other patients went to the first floor for some entertainment that had been arranged by an outside group. I seized the opportunity to witness to the bedfast gentleman, who had a brain tumor. He accepted Christ and insisted I write his sister and tell her. He wasn't satisfied until I had prepared the letter to mail. Sometime during the night he fell out of bed. He was rushed to the Kansas City Veterans' Hospital because it had the necessary equipment and surgeons for his particular need. Just before being discharged from Wadsworth, I received a letter from his sister. Her brother had died during surgery. She wrote that most of the family were active Christians, and her brother's lost condition had been a great concern to the family for years. She further stated that the minister who officiated at her brother's funeral read my letter during the services. She wrote, "It turned a sad occasion into a service of victory!"

Often a negative approach may be used to make something more understandable. Should you think that because this man was won to Christ, my illness at Wadsworth was bearing my cross, I believe you are wrong. I received nothing but joy from the experience. There was no persecution suffered for Christ's sake because of what took place. I did not volunteer to go to the hospital. Now, we could all agree that the Lord had one of His witnesses in the right place at the right time, and I was fortunate enough to be the one.

So if this experience was not bearing my cross, how much less is it not bearing our cross because we happen to have a hangnail, stomachache, or some really serious illness? Please don't declare that my backache is just the cross I have to bear. Save it for those who set aside their own plans to follow and obey Jesus, even to the ends of the earth. When I surrendered to preach, turned my back on Sears and some

23

other things, and became ready to go where He wished in order to win souls, that was taking up my cross. I've been carrying it, often very poorly, ever since. Remember, the Cross is the symbol of a sacrificed life, and one sacrificed so that others may be saved!

Suffering—God's Punishment

A brother pastor once offered approximately this. "It is my belief that sickness and suffering are some of the ways our Heavenly Father takes His disobedient children to the woodshed. He does it for their own good. The lines of communication are blocked with their sins. If they will seek out their sins, confess and forsake them, they will immediately be back in God's favor. He will hear them, heal them, and use them."

Shades of poor old Job! When we boil it all down, Job's three "comforting" friends had the same basic message: "Job, you have no doubt committed some great sin. You have made God angry, and He is punishing you. Confess your sin, and He will relieve you of your agony."

This idea may be conveyed in numerous ways, but it always comes out the same. It can often be attributed to a Pharisee complex, meaning one with an overinflated, self-righteous, superiority complex. In what little time is now available to spend with church groups, I continue to encounter this attitude dressed in various costumes. One might say God is represented as having candy in one hand and a whip in the other one. If one pleases God, one is given the candy; if one displeases Him, one gets the whip. Some even seem to believe God delivers either one with similar emotions. He is sometimes pictured as something of a sadist who enjoys measuring out punishment upon those He loves.

I am a father. I have walked the floor with every one of our five children when they have been sick. I have prayed for them, hurt for them, even prayed to be allowed to suffer their illnesses for them. This more nearly fits my conception of God. Oh, yes, such feelings cannot be compared with His in degree, but they may be compared in kind or direction. Whether He ever heals me or not, He is concerned for me and suffers because I suffer. One who does not accept this does not have much of a faith to sustain him in difficult times. The child who has a close relationship with his parents during the day finds their presence even more assuring in the dark.

Job's wife must have given Job a strange kind of "comfort." Her alternative to Job's friends' advice was to "curse God, and die" (2:9). I thank God for the caring, encouraging, supportive kind of wife He gave me long before I had any idea of needing such a helpmeet. Frankly, I could never have made it this far with Job's kind of wife.

Satan's Affliction—Faith Can Heal

Quite often some church members are also faithful followers of television and radio healing ministries. Usually one of their greatest desires is that their pastors and local churches pattern their services along healing lines. Surely, having a pastor with a chronic illness must seem a golden opportunity. When calling on the sick, they seem to say, in various ways, "You have not exercised enough faith to be healed. We know all sickness comes from Satan. If you can just muster enough faith, God will cast him out, and you will be healed."

There has never been any doubt in my mind about God's power to heal. He is the Great Physician, and ultimately all healing does come from Him. Whether it be in the medicines contained in the raw materials of this planet for man to discover, in the intelligence and skills He has given certain people to use what He has made available, or by His actual intervention in human history, it is still from Him. I have prayed for His healing power, both for others and myself, far more times than can be counted, but have also prayed that His guidance would be given to the doctors for correct and effective treatment.

Healing faith has some amazing aspects. One time a group of people prayed that I might have the faith to be healed. There was no question of my need of it. However, I asked them to remember an incident recorded in Mark 2 where four men carried a man, sick of the palsy, and let him down through the roof for Jesus to heal. The Bible states, "When Jesus saw *their* faith" (v. 5, italics added), His power became operative in the sick man. In John 9, Jesus healed a blind man who didn't even know who He was. It is enough to challenge any serious student of the Bible

Most healing evangelists have not impressed me favorably. I've always been more supportive of the Billy Graham type. During the first three years in my final pastorate, however, I was led to think very seriously about a healing ministry. People have often suggested that, as one being in pain, I might be better able to understand and minister to the sick. I usually felt this was an attempt to explain why healing has always seemed to elude me. Often I wondered if I was an embarrassment to the Christian community.

I had been in my new pastorate only two weeks when a lady called the home where I was living, leaving a message that her husband was in the hospital. As soon as I received it, I left immediately, arriving just in time to be with the couple when their doctor told them the test indicated serious surgery was needed. It was good that I was there and could pray with them immediately.

My temporary lodging was with a lovely church family until I could arrange for a residence and bring my family from Arizona. The man of the house owned a share in a small plane, and he suggested we both take three days off, fly back to our home in Arizona, and visit my family. On the return trip I felt an urgency to be at the hospital. After landing, I drove directly to the hospital from the airport. I was with the family less than five minutes when they were told it was cancer. It was more than coincidence that I flew almost 500 miles, drove through several miles of traffic, and arrived at that time. Again it was at the time of their greatest need of their pastor. I began to wonder if a future ministry was somehow bound up with this cancer victim.

The third special time was one morning when I was walking down the hall to the patient's room. The surgeon and the patient's wife were talking in the hallway. The wife motioned for me to join them. In a moment the doctor said, "I have recently had three other patients just like your husband."

"What happened to them?" the wife asked.

"They died! You might as well accept it because we have done all medical science can do," replied the doctor bluntly. His gruffness was hard to understand but perhaps he knew that the wife was a strong woman and could handle it. He may have been trying to force her to face what he thought was reality. She, on the other hand, was determined not to give up her husband.

After the doctor left us, she declared that he had never given her husband a chance. He had prostate cancer and had delayed far too long to have an examination. It was time to pray with her again.

On the 63rd day of her husband's hospitalization I received an early morning call from the wife. "Will you go to the hospital and anoint my husband with oil?" she asked.

This was the first time I had ever been asked to do such a thing. I kept her talking while I frantically turned to James 5:14. "Is any sick among you? let him call for the elders of the church; and let them pray over him, anointing him with oil in the name of the Lord." That scripture has been explained in a number of ways, but I knew none of them would satisfy her.

Quickly I decided it was easier to do it than to try to explain it away. After all, it sounded quite plain. "Now listen to me," I said. "I'll do it if you and your husband will understand that neither the oil nor I can heal him. Only God can do that! I will anoint him as an act of obedience to the Scriptures, and we will trust the Lord to bless our faith."

She agreed, and so did her husband when we got to the hospital. She had brought a small bottle of olive oil. I made a little talk about faith and obedience, marked a cross on the patient's head with the oil, and prayed as hard as I knew how.

The next day the doctor came in and examined him. "Something's happened here," he said. "This man has been healed!" The next morning the doctor checked him again and began pulling tubes out of him. He told him that if he was still doing well by Friday, he would send him home.

You interpret this event any way you wish, but this couple said the next two years were the happiest of their lives. He had absolutely no pain and was not restricted in any way. They did some traveling and even went to the Holy Land. Their doctor was an atheist. Some months later he said he felt like he should genuflect every time he passed that room because surely divine healing had taken place there.

Within a few weeks two more spectacular healings of cancer occurred. One involved the real estate agent who sold us our residence. He had a similar cancer and radical surgery. The other was a young man who later became our minister of music. His doctors said his tumor had metastasized, and they gave us no hope. This young man is happily serving the Lord today with no evidence of malignancy.

Several more amazing healings took place during this period of time. One afternoon, soon after we arrived at our church, information came about one of the oldest church members who was quite ill. She was living with one daughter, and a second had come from another state to help. On calling in the home, I found the sick lady conscious and alert.

That was the last time we ever spoke together. I called almost every day, but she was in a coma for weeks. Both daughters claimed, and indeed it was very evident, that she would be moaning and restless; but when I placed my hand on her forehead and prayed, she would become quiet and relaxed. Strangely, she failed to do this even for other pastors. I was with her when she quietly passed away.

A few of the older women in our church maintained a telephone prayer group. They probably believed more in prayer than any other group in the church. One morning one of the ladies called another of the prayer warriors with an especially pressing request. In the conversation, she asked the other lady if she would ask me to pray about a matter. "I will," said the other lady, "but you want to be sure about what you request of him. When he prays, things happen."

This was heady stuff. It is the kind of thing that might cause a young pastor, or an old fool, to get carried away. After all, we are only human. Frankly, I had always felt my prayer life was weak; too little time was spent on my knees. Nevertheless, my ministry had to be reevaluated. Did God want me to join the ranks of the healers? If so, why had He not healed me? I considered myself an evangelistic preacher and church builder. How could I honestly give myself to something that was so foreign to my normal manner and procedure? These questions had not been seriously considered before because I had never really been involved in such events.

After much agonizing in prayer, I concluded the Lord was doing some unusual things among us because He wanted a troubled congregation to know He was still in their midst. He had left little doubt of His power and concern. I told Him I would willingly give myself to be used as He wished, that I would take care not to hinder in any way, but that I would carry on my usual ministry unless He made it clear that it was not His will. There are those on both sides of the divine healing issue who will be critical of my thoughts, actions, and decisions, but I am at peace with the Lord concerning the matter.

God's Blessing—Thank Him

Some Christians are sure all sickness comes from Satan. Others are just as certain it all is given to us by God. Moreover, the latter say we should constantly thank God for causing us to suffer. He knows what is best for us; therefore, we should praise and love Him more than ever for giving us the experience. Have you ever tried thanking God in the process of passing a kidney stone or a gallstone? How about during a vicious attack of shingles or with a freshly herniated disk in your spine? This is not meant to ridicule those who can. Indeed, they deserve great respect for their perseverance. All the ailments mentioned have been a part of my experience, but during those times it was very hard even to concentrate on prayer. Paul wrote, "In every thing give thanks" (1 Thess. 5:18). Many of us have used this as a text a number of times. After hurting, however, for 24 hours a day, 365 days a year, and over 21 years at this point, one's praise often seems more feeble than one's prayers. Such thoughts as "every good gift and every perfect gift is from above" comes more readily to mind (James 1:17). One may feel more like Paul must have felt when he prayed three times for the removal of the thorn in his flesh. God did not remove the thorn but told Paul His grace was sufficient for him to bear it (2 Cor. 12:9). Young Timothy apparently had stomach trouble (1 Tim. 5:23). Epaphroditus almost died in Rome (Phil. 2:25-30). Paul commended him for his devotion. It can become very difficult not to want to blame someone or something for pain. Sometimes I want to blame Satan. God forbid that I should ever feel any bitterness toward the Lord again. I'm certain, if God should allow us to suffer pain, He has our ultimate good as His objective.

30

Preparation for Special Service

A denominational worker, who is also a good friend, once said to me, "I believe you have been chosen to suffer for Christ's sake. God knows you have the strength to endure it, even as Job did, and He is doubtlessly preparing you for some special service." It would be wonderful if he had been correct; but since I am now past the age of retirement, and still nearly bedfast, I have obviously disappointed this friend.

In trying to understand the omniscience of God (and most of us cannot see beyond the end of our noses prophetically), I must realize He could still have some special service in mind for me. If so, I think He should hurry because time is becoming short. I find myself wishing for the truth and application of Matthew Henry's statement: "Extraordinary afflictions are not always the punishment of extraordinary sins, but sometimes the trials of extraordinary graces. Sanctified afflictions are spiritual promotions."

Suffering—Beyond Understanding

Finally, there are those visitors who keep repeating, "I just can't understand it, I just can't understand it." This is usually followed with suggestions that a servant of God should never be sick or injured and that the world needs every person of God on the job. Others give their brand of wisdom: "I just can't understand why God would let His called men be sick"; then adding another twist of the noose, "I know a fellow who had the same operation, and he was back to work in half the time," they finally go on their cheerful way. The thing I just can't understand is why God permits them to make calls on the sick!

Most readers can identify somewhere along the way with some of these half-dozen examples. This is not meant to discourage those who are willing to invest their time calling

31

on the sick. Those who have visited me over the years have been appreciated, and I have tried to make visiting the sick a high priority in my own ministry. My concern is that we bring comfort and encouragement to the patient rather than hurt and confusion. Our work would profit from a well-taught course, on a periodic basis, on visiting the sick, suffering, and disabled. This is something every pastor and every church should consider.

I have been able to cope with the diversity of doctrines and the hurtful statements often not understood by those who spoke them. I have listened to church and personal problems piled on my sickbed, the unavoidable guilt trips, and the gossip, usually more bad than good, left behind to think on long after the visitors are gone. But what about new Christians, and those who still are little beyond babes in Christ? Are we supposed to comfort, confuse, or condemn them? How can we help them when we throw so many conflicting ideas at them? What a blessing are those concerned callers who are able to communicate genuine solicitude and love, speak briefly of God's knowledge and care, suppress discouraging news, offer sincere prayer, and soon find their way out of the patient's room. Yes, it would be well worth all the time and trouble to present a church study and produce some more visitors such as these. Then we would surely comfort those who suffer and help hasten their recovery, rather than confuse them or seem even to condemn them for allowing themselves to be sick and taking too much time to recover.

To summarize the six negative types:
1. Your pain and illness is simply the cross you must bear.
2. Your suffering is God's punishment for your sins.
3. Your affliction is from Satan; have faith to cast him out.
4. Your suffering is a blessing from God; thank Him for it.
5. Your suffering is a preparation for some special service.

6. Your sickness is beyond understanding. Why should a Christian worker suffer?

   You may feel some of these still have valid application. If so, please be very, very careful when and how you use them. Give time to meditation and prayer before you enter that sickroom.

3

From Birth Through Rebirth

The main purpose of this chapter is to reveal the things that affected my principal illness from birth. My salvation experience is included so that the reader may examine it for reasons why other prayers for healing have not been granted. Hopefully we will come to a better understanding, or at least peace of mind, as to why the Lord has not miraculously healed me, and why I've continued to suffer more than most with bone fusion problems.

As I had indicated to my wife during our trip to the hospital, I would have several days to think and pray about applying for disability coverage. I thought mostly about the past and prayed about the future. It was necessary to do both.

Sharing these things should not be misconstrued as complaining. I have not missed out on any significant portion of life. There are multiplied numbers of people who have had to live with pain.

Life began for me on a farm in northern Missouri, the youngest of five children. My father and mother were considerably older than the average parents when I was born. Since Mother had worn dentures for some time, she was probably unaware that her pregnancies had robbed her body of the calcium she needed in larger quantities during those months.

At birth there was an immediate crisis. I was allergic to my mother's milk, cow's milk, goat's milk, and any formula the doctor concocted. Being a 12-pounder, I had a little surplus fat on which to live. (However, I was also an instrument baby and received a cracked skull in the process of birth.) Finally it was discovered I could tolerate a thick, sweet, canned milk named Eagle Brand. I became a sugar junkie as an infant. As a growing child, I refused to drink milk or eat food that supplied calcium and lime. In fact, I have never cared for milk but have always had an insatiable sweet tooth.

Speaking of teeth brings to mind another continuing problem. Both my baby and permanent teeth were soft and chalky. As a small child I sat on Mother's lap and cried for teeth like her dentures so that they wouldn't ache.

My baby teeth had such long and deformed roots, they had to be pulled. Our local dentist persuaded my parents to take me to a dentist in the city for special treatment when I was about six years old. He was afraid the roots of the baby teeth would damage the permanent ones. After a general anesthetic, most of the baby teeth were removed. Only one permanent molar was damaged, and it had come in without protective enamel. Another dentist tried to pull it later, but it crumbled and had to be taken out in pieces. He abandoned one root, and I still carry it in my lower left jawbone.

At 13 years of age, my parents made an all-day appointment to have my cavities filled. The process began at 8 A.M. and continued until after dark. A total of 21 fillings, with 8 gold fillings in the upper front teeth, were completed that day. The dentist guaranteed the gold fillings for 25 years, but they began to loosen in 1 year. We returned to the dentist's office only to find he had died. The guarantee was buried with him.

The toothaches seemed to be endless, but I did not have to wait long for dentures. The first ones came at age 19.

On the last day of high school, the classmate who was to become my wife within another year accompanied me to a naval recruiting center where I attempted to join the navy. Work was hard to find, and I thought I wanted to make a career in the military service. After one look at my teeth, those conducting the testing turned me down. Later in 1944, after I had a wife, two children, and a set of dentures, I enlisted as an air cadet under what was called voluntary induction. There was no trouble this time! My teeth received a grade of 1, the best mark the armed forces gave.

To deviate somewhat from the main purpose of this chapter, anyone wearing dentures almost always has his embarrassing/humorous-in-retrospect moments. Because of the bone condition, my gums shrink more rapidly than the average person's. This has made it necessary to be fitted with new dentures frequently. With so many sets available, I've usually kept a couple in a clothing drawer for emergencies.

One Sunday a fine young adult couple joined our church. They had three children, two of whom were five-year-old twin girls. The following Sunday the family was invited to our house for dinner. Just before the evening services I saw the little girls playing with a set of dentures in the foyer. They looked all too familiar, so I eased over beside the girls and quietly suggested they give them to me. "They're ours. We bought them from your boy," one answered far too loudly. "We gave him a whole dime for them," insisted the other. As the early arrivers watched with interest and humor, I blushed like a schoolboy. Finally I managed to get the girls out of sight and gave them a good profit on their purchase.

After church, my own five-year-old was instructed more fully about such things!

As long as my body would stand it, I used many gestures and tried to maintain eye contact with all groups when I preached. The choir sat behind me in the Independence church but were seated to my right when I first went to Colorado. One morning I pronounced a rather explosive word, with considerable volume, and felt the upper dentures come loose. I threw my right hand up over my mouth, spun to the left, caught the teeth, and had them back in place at 180 degrees. Fearing to complete the circle because I didn't want to face the choir, I turned back the way I had first turned. Nobody seemed to notice what had really happened. On the way home Doris observed, "You forgot the choir wasn't behind you this morning, didn't you?" I just grunted something that sounded like "Yeah" and never pursued the matter.

Early problems for me were more extensive than just teeth. The leg aches were terrible. They seemed completely unrelated to any physical activity. There were many days when I would sit in front of the kitchen wood range with feet and legs propped up in the oven, trying not to cry. Father and Mother said these were just growing pains. If that had been true, I should still be growing because the pains are still frequent.

Somewhere in my teens our family doctor told me I had suffered from rickets or rachitis. This seemed strange because I was taller than most boys my age and had reached my lifetime height by age 14. Apparently the bones were soft, just as the teeth were.

I was very active on the farm and in sports through grade school. In fact, I had been a full-fledged field hand since the age of 10. I was pitched, or fell, from the back of a horse or steer more times than can be remembered. On one such occasion I received severe ligament damage but no broken bones. My left arm was in a sling for several weeks. Another time I rode my saddle mare at a dead run, on a rutted and frozen road, downhill. It was a very foolish thing to do. The mare fell, and I was catapulted over her head, landing on my arms, face, and chest. The frozen road tore and bruised me, but I had no broken bones. It was like a miracle, but the mare escaped injury too.

One of my favorite pastimes was to slip up on the mare while she was grazing, jump on her back, and without saddle and bridle, beat a tattoo on her ribs with my heels and ride at full speed. She was as mischievous as I and would try to unload me at every opportunity. One day she dragged me off by scraping her side against a tree. My leg was badly bruised, but again, no bones were broken. Another time when I tried this trick, she ran to the barnyard. Water from a recent rainstorm was standing in a low place in the gate. She had to turn when she ran through the gate opening, and her legs slipped from under her. I flew over her head and landed on both feet. The fall knocked the wind out of the mare, but I was unscathed. Another opportunity to break bones passed by. While on the farm I was always climbing trees, building tree houses, or fixing vines or ropes to swing across hollows. It was unnatural that I should escape without broken bones, but that was the case.

Soon after obtaining a driver's license, I rolled a car several times at a very high speed. Common sense would have predicted my ending up on a mortician's slab. Although I was unconscious for a while, the doctor only had to suture a cut on my side and tape my ribs. One thing that happened at that time may have related to future spinal problems. My coccyx, or tailbone, was very painful and tender for a few months. It has been crooked since that time.

*　　*　　*

Employment was difficult to find during the Great Depression. Now married, I had a lifetime scholarship to a business college but soon had to drop out because of our economic situation. At 19, the only work I could find was in the government program, WPA. A very proud young man, I resented the criticism that WPA workers were lazy. People poked fun at us and said the government intended to install rope handles in our shovels so that we couldn't lean on them. Of course we couldn't have done any work with them either.

That winter I worked in a rock quarry. Each one in our group had a large wheelbarrow, a sledgehammer, and a flat-bottomed shovel. We broke the rock down to a size we could lift into the wheelbarrow, scooped up the smaller pieces, and made a run to the rock crusher with our load. We had to gather as much speed as possible because we had to push our loads up a rather steep incline, made with two-inch lumber, and dump it into the hopper of the crusher. I always tried to handle the biggest load because pride brought fear of public opinion.

One morning, as I started to get out of bed, the ball of my left foot felt like I had stepped on a coal of fire. Lifting my leg back on the bed caused the pain to cease. Again I tried to arise, but as soon as my foot touched the floor, the terrible pain returned. After several unsuccessful attempts I asked Doris to call the foreman and tell him I couldn't work that day. Later in the day, I managed to hobble to the doctor's office. His diagnosis was that I had frozen the foot. I didn't know enough to dispute him, and it was a severely cold winter. His prognosis was that I would have recurring attacks of pain for some time. Years later it was discovered that my spine had been injured. It was my first herniated disk, and the pain in the foot was caused by pressure on certain nerves in my back.

For several years I had occasional trouble with both the foot and my back. We moved to Kansas City in 1941, and I acquired a job with Sears, Roebuck and Company. Sometimes I had to miss a day of work, but absenteeism was kept to a minimum. My two year stint in the armed forces occurred during this time. I made it through that ordeal and returned to Sears after the war. Soon I was given charge of a floor. The job of my dreams was buying merchandise. The company was organized into three major divisions: operating, merchandising, and sales. I felt somewhat discouraged because of working in the Operating Division, when the big dream was a job in merchandising. It would stray too far from my purpose to tell how it all came about, but beginning on the first working day of 1948, I received that coveted dream job. I was a merchandise buyer, with a good chance for advancement, and had a sitting-down job. Finally, my life from birth seemed to hold some promise. Little did I realize the desperate need of another birth.

My new birth happened seven months after becoming a buyer. About this time, a chain of events began to happen in our family. Our two older children started to Sunday School. It created little problem, since the church was close enough for them to walk. It wasn't very long until our little daughter began insisting that we have prayer before meals. To keep the peace, we agreed and assigned the task to her. Secretly I began praying again. We often went driving on Sunday evenings, and when we would pass a church, either my wife or I would say, "You know, we all should get started to church." In July 1948, the church where our children attended Sunday School had two weeks of revival services. Our daughter went forward on the middle Sunday morning and asked to be baptized.

That afternoon two ladies from the church visited in our home. I hid in our bedroom. They asked Doris about permission for our daughter's baptism. She told them she didn't know much about such things but felt we would not stand in the child's way. They departed with the assurance everything would be well, and left an invitation to attend the meetings.

"You shouldn't have encouraged them about baptizing

Anna," were my first words upon coming out of the hiding place. "You don't know what she may be getting into."

"Well, we can find out," Doris answered. "They invited us to their services."

We talked it over, and I finally decided to attend if I could get my hard-drinking neighbor to accompany us. His wife and mine were good friends, but I didn't think he would go. When I asked him, he readily agreed to go with us on Thursday night. I thought this was good because he always came home intoxicated every Friday night.

Despite my misgivings, Thursday finally arrived. We were all ready for church when it became apparent our neighbor had decided to spend the night drinking. I decided to take my family anyway and take my chances on what might happen. I was really nervous because I had never attended church services except for a few times as a child. Some weeks later one of the deacons, who was greeting people in the foyer that night, said he was sure I was a visiting preacher. Had I known that, I would have been more at ease. I herded my family into a back pew, and the services soon began.

I don't remember much about that meeting. But I did understand, for the first time, that I was lost and that Jesus would save me. During the invitation, another deacon stepped up and asked, "Are you a Christian?"

"I guess not," I replied.

"Wouldn't you like to go forward and become one?"

"No, sir! I don't jump into things I'm not sure about," I said firmly. He just smiled and stepped back against the wall.

That night I didn't sleep well. I didn't work well the next day either. My main activities consisted of smoking and drumming my fingers on the top of the desk. I couldn't understand it, but I was in misery. The conviction of the Holy Spirit is an awesome thing with which to deal. I left work before the rush because, since I was accomplishing nothing,

I might as well be miserable at home. I had no appetite at dinner. Later, Doris was astonished when I asked, "Would you like to go back to the revival tonight?" She wanted to but had not felt it was wise to ask.

Again I don't remember much about the service, but I knew what I wanted. When the evangelist concluded his message, I did not wait for the singing of the invitation hymn. I didn't know that was the usual thing to do. There was a wide center aisle of freshly waxed and polished hardwood. Under the reflection of the lights, it looked like a "great white way." Yet it felt somewhat like wading in knee-deep mud because the effort to reach the front was so difficult. I fell on my knees and talked and prayed with a Christian worker. I confessed faith in Christ as my personal Savior. After I had made my decision, I looked around and saw my wife on one side and our little boy on the other side. Instead of one, there were four of our family baptized the following Sunday afternoon.

This chapter cannot be closed without reporting that our alcoholic neighbor was saved a few years later. He quit drinking and became quite involved in the life of the church. God called him home some time ago. Although we found Christ before he did, he has beaten us to heaven.

4

From Rebirth to Retirement

In chapter 1 I mentioned accepting Christ at age 28, the whirlwind of church activity that then engulfed us, and my surrender to the ministry a year later. I was still a young man but felt very far behind in education and experience. I jumped into a four-year college program with both feet and, with summer sessions plus a heavy regular schedule, graduated in 27 months. Seminary work began in the fall, after graduation from college, but I decelerated school progress to accommodate more church and denominational work.

During the first 15 months in the pastorate, I pastored two churches simultaneously. Then I accepted the call of a church in the Independence, Mo., area where I served nine and one-half years and finished both college and seminary. The church completed a two-phase building program and a number of successful financial programs. We may not write much here about the number of people who were saved, baptized, and otherwise added to the church, because of poor personal records kept; but in all my pastorates people were reached for Christ at a more rapid rate when the church was building, raising money, or striving to go forward in other ways. Congregations should never fear that their evangelistic thrust will be blunted by sincere efforts in other areas of church need. More and more time was spent outside our own church in revivals, helping other churches with their financial programs, teaching the fundamentals of our boys' work, teaching courses on the service of deacons, teaching Bible courses, serving as youth camp director, serving our association as moderator, plus various other offices and as a member of numerous committees.

The Lord taught many lessons during this period, and two of them closely related my health to the ministry. The first occurred when I entered the hospital for major but routine surgery. All went well after the surgery until I had been back in my room for a couple of hours. Suddenly I became very ill, went into a coma for over three and one-half days, and frightened everyone, including the doctors. Our church came together on Thursday evening to have special prayer for me. I awoke from the coma at 9 P.M. that same evening, just as they were concluding their prayer service. Recovery from that time on was rapid. Was this just a coincidence? Hardly! What had been wrong with me? Nobody knew. Years later we decided it might have been an allergic reaction to Demerol. What's the difference? God taught us that "the prayer of faith shall save the sick" (James 5:15), and that He does intervene in the affairs of mankind.

The second of the two lessons came when I was 38 years old. It happened during the most active period of my life in both the local church and in denominational work. It was diagnosed as a myocardial infarction thought due to a coronary occlusion. In other words, a heart attack. I was supposed to die. At least that was what the doctors told my wife. I was

44

in I.C.U. for 14 days and I spent a total of 29 days in the hospital. The lesson? God has *not* built a hedge about His own (see Job 1:10). Even Christians, doing Christian work, are still subject to the limitations of their human flesh.

After this experience, the church came together and demanded that I take at least one day off per week and do this regularly from that time forward. "You may have any day you want," they stated. "Well," I replied, "if I can have any day, I guess I'll take Sunday." Sunday really was the favorite day in my workweek. It is difficult for a pastor to have a certain day of the week completely off, but I am convinced he will be a better pastor for it.

For a few years some trouble persisted with my heart and circulation, but the heart is fine now. High altitudes are still a bother, but nothing else causes discomfort. There is a damaged area within the heart, but I'm no more subject to another attack than anyone else. Yes, God certainly can heal, but He expects us to use the sense He has given us to care for our bodies.

A heart attack is an effective way to dispose of a bunch of responsibilities. Work outside the local church was cut to a minimum. It was much easier to accept a call to be the pastor of a church in Grand Junction, Colo. Of course, by this time I had resumed a normal load as a pastor. Although it was easier to leave the denominational work, it was not easy to leave the people at Independence. That work was my longest period of service in any one church, and our friends were many.

After moving, I again threw myself with abandon into the work of the local church, the association, and the state convention. Really, it seemed that the Lord's second lesson had taught me very little. I have often wondered if I exasperated Him when I thought I was pleasing Him.

The busy life continued. From October 1961 through January of 1969, I served in Grand Junction. The mission in

Montrose constructed a new building in 1962. The Spanish Mission in Grand Junction completed one in 1964, and the mother church finished an all-new church plant in 1966. The mother church sold the old building, purchased eight and one-half acres of land at a prominent intersection, and built a beautiful building that housed both worship and educational facilities. Outside the local church I served the state convention as boys' work director (volunteer), boys' camp director, six years as an executive board member including time as both chairman and vice-chairman, and as a member of various committees. I served our association of churches as moderator for three years, as youth camp director, and in other jobs and on most committees. Positions of leadership in the local ministerial alliance became a part of my schedule, and once, during a period when the office was vacant, I served for several months as volunteer chaplain for the local VA Hospital. I accepted one revival back in Missouri each year; others in Colorado, New Mexico, and California; and one in Australia, which resulted in a trip around the world and a good visit to the Holy Land. These things are mentioned so that you may know I was busy about the Lord's work. This was a very happy period, and it made my life even more difficult to bear after such a limiting affliction came upon me approximately in the middle of my Colorado ministry.

In May 1965, while carrying a wide carriage typewriter, I fell and landed on my lower back. All the previous back trouble immediately returned. For the first time I realized what had caused the sensation of a coal of fire on the ball of my left foot so many years before. In addition to the old symptoms, a numbness was added to a large part of the left leg. At times I could not sense what position my left foot was in, and a number of falls resulted. Our standard shift cars had to be traded for those with automatic transmissions. Occasionally it became necessary to spend some days in bed.

Every kind of doctor available in Grand Junction was contacted, but there was no relief. My left leg became about one and one-half inches shorter than the right one. Finally, on a return visit to our family physician, he indicated it was useless to give further treatment unless I would enter the hospital for tests. I agreed and found, in addition to the tests, there was to be 10 days of traction plus a myelogram. This is a special kind of X ray taken after the spinal fluid has been replaced by a heavy dye.

After the myelogram, the doctor brought the films for me to see. They showed a herniated disk, in the lumbar region, pressing against certain nerves. He advised that he might "buy some time" with the traction, but there was no guarantee about how long. The only permanent treatment was surgery. (After paying the hospital bill, I concluded I was the one who had bought the time!) He advised going to the Mayo Clinic for surgery, but I did not feel up to traveling so far from home. An appointment was set up with one of two orthopedic teams in the area. They acquired the myelogram from the hospital and surgery was the verdict of the doctor assigned to the case. His alternative was eventually an atrophied left leg and a wheelchair. His time of surgery was as soon as I felt that the pain was no longer bearable.

After about three months I decided we had waited long enough and called the surgeon. He immediately made the arrangements. A laminectomy was performed in January of 1967. Everything seemed to go well at first. The surgeon pointed out that I had been suffering from an old injury, dating from youth. He said it had fused naturally, but it had broken loose when I fell with the typewriter. During surgery he cleaned out the calcium pile and what was left of the herniated disk. He also advised that I had considerable deterioration of the spine.

I had anticipated being well or, at least, much better. Wrong! Wrong! Wrong! Now I had varying degrees of pain 24 hours per day. Relief came only with potent pain pills and strong sleeping pills. Within a couple of months I was hospitalized again for 36 days. Still no relief. The doctor suggested a trip to Glenwood Springs to bathe in the hot mineral waters for a few weeks. Although it was only 180 miles round trip, the effort did me more harm than the waters did good. A pulpit supply was arranged with the church, and we moved up to the Springs for a month. While in the water I felt better, but there was no lasting relief.

After a few weeks back in the pulpit, I requested a leave of absence. I took my two weeks vacation and furnished pulpit supply for another two weeks. We went back to Missouri, to Doris's mother's home. There I did little but lie in bed and walk, but again there was no relief.

We went back to Grand Junction, and I did the best I could. The people were good to understand. We had moved into our new church building before the surgery. Things were going well with frequent additions to the membership. Nevertheless, I began to feel the church needed a pastor who could give more than I. Doris and I discussed this many times. After one especially cold winter and the beginning of another, we began to pray that the Lord might move us to a warmer climate and a smaller church. We even came to the place where we prayed He might move us to Arizona. Of course we always added, "If You can find it in Your will."

This was a somewhat complicated request, but it was answered in an unusually precise manner. I was engaged in a revival effort in Albuquerque, N.Mex., when the call came. The evening meetings were early, and I had gone directly to bed after reaching the pastor's home and taking heavy medication for both pain and sleep. The pastor awakened me around ten o'clock; a telephone was in his hands. "He says it's important," the pastor explained apologetically. Hardly able to think or talk, I took the phone. The chairman of the pulpit committee of a church in Sedona, Ariz., was on the line. The

Sedona congregation was interested in having me preach for them in view of a call. Somehow I managed to tell him I would come. (I've often wondered what he thought was wrong with me, but I never did ask him.) The church called me to be their pastor, and convinced God had answered our prayers, I accepted.

Sedona was a small, but rapidly growing, retirement and resort area. It was a very beautiful place. We felt as if we were living in a national park. Although the church was much smaller, it had a lovely building. The people were very good to support us. Our domestic mission organization, on the national level, helped us financially for some time because of the resort nature of the area. I'm sure this would never have happened but for a friend who had moved up to that level of service. After visiting with us, he immediately saw the qualifications of the field.

A local doctor did all he could to help me cope with the pain. He tried shooting cortisone and Novocain directly into the injured area, but with no lasting results. He also added the drug Percodan, which was to cause me much trouble. The recommended dose was not enough to stop the pain, so I began skipping doses and then doubling up so that I could experience some relief some of the time. I also persuaded the doctor to increase the doses after a while. Finally one day I told him something more had to be done. Regardless of the temperature, I was always in a cold sweat. He reached over and placed his hand on my forehead. "Man, I didn't realize you were suffering so much. I want to send you to an orthopedic specialist as soon as possible."

"Well, send me to the best," I said. "A poor one costs just as much as a good one."

After checking out a Phoenix specialist with four other doctors in Flagstaff and Cottonwood, he made an appointment for me with him. I will never forget my initial contact with this doctor. After arriving for the appointment, I was placed in a small examining room. In a few minutes a very dapper, middle-aged man strode in and sort of barked, "Well, what's your story?"

"What do you mean, my story?" I asked.

"Everyone who has a back problem has a story," he said. "We might as well get yours out of the way."

His attitude irritated me more than his words. I almost walked out without saying any more. Standing and looking at him, I finally said, "Doctor, I've driven over 120 miles this morning to seek your advice. Now, if you don't want to examine me, there are other doctors who will."

"Let's not get huffy now," he responded. "First we'll need some X rays so that we'll know what we're dealing with. I'll take you to X ray, and when they're done with you, come back here."

This procedure was followed. When the doctor returned to the examining room, he seemed like a different person. He was probably pestered with his share of frauds, trying to sue somebody or get out of work. In fact, we became good friends over a period of time. He sat on a gurney beside me and pointed out that the X rays indicated at least three vertebrae were jammed together. He wanted to place me into a full body cast for a month. He asked if there was another driver with me. When he learned there was none, his nurse phoned our Sunday School superintendent. He, and another man who did not belong to our church, came. The body cast extended from just above the knees to high up under my arms. It was so cold I thought it would never reach normal body temperature. I was to see him again in two weeks at a clinic he, and the other members of the firm, held in Cottonwood once each month.

The fellows helped me home that night, and later I was able to carry on most of my work because one of our cars had a reclining driver's seat. I did my own preaching, but it was inconvenient not to be able to sit down. The body cast was awkward, but it relieved so much of the pain that I didn't mind. I didn't know what I would be given to replace the cast, because it would have been ridiculous going through life wearing such a thing; but I felt sure this indicated that some kind of apparatus would bring relief.

The doctor, however, when we talked in the Cottonwood clinic, told me he was only trying to determine if I was a candidate for a fusion. The body cast had stabilized the spine, and fusing the vertebrae should do the same thing. In other words, it was proven to him that the surgery was needed. I mentioned that the surgeons in Grand Junction would not fuse anyone over 45. He replied that he did not like to, but my vital signs were those of a much younger man. It was decided that I would go to the Phoenix clinic in two more weeks for the removal of the cast. From there I would enter the hospital for more surgery.

The evening before the operation, the doctor stated that it would feel as though a big Mack truck had hit me. Upon first seeing him after the surgery, I asked him if he had noted the license number. He said that he felt the surgery was successful but that there was a general deterioration up and down the spine. "You need a spinal transplant," he affirmed. "Too bad medical science hasn't developed that procedure."

The next seven months and one week were spent in bed, with the exception of approximately one hour each day for exercises. The same two men who came to Phoenix when I was placed in the body cast came for me after the 21-day hospital stay. The one who was not a member of our church owned a Dodge motor home. They simply put me to bed in it and drove me home. Each month I had to go to the Cottonwood Hospital and was driven there in the motor home the entire seven months.

When I told the doctor about needing to get back to work, he said some things that caused concern about my condition. For instance, he noted, "Those bones in your back

51

are quite soft. I should know; I worked on them." Again he said, "You may be 100 percent disabled as far as I can tell. You will have to decide when you are able to resume your work." I have often wondered if he was trying to convey something about the feasibility of ever returning to work again. Perhaps I should have sought disability status at that time.

Soon after, a church on the West Coast extended a pastoral call. I did not want to leave Arizona. The people had been so good to us. After being sure concerning the need for another operation on the spine, I had sent the church a letter of resignation. It did not seem right to leave the congregation without an undershepherd for so long. But they would not accept my resignation! In fact, they paid the full salary and allowances for the lengthy period that it was necessary to lie in bed. They acquired the help of one of our state convention workers and also paid his expenses. Most of the people, when they came to visit, brought something to eat. Amazingly our attendance stayed up well. The people accepted my illness as a real challenge that the church needed. There were lost people who came to talk with me about Christ and church membership, people who had failed to move their church membership when they had moved from other areas, and people from other denominations. The hospital bed was placed in our living room where I could see through the glass of the front door. When people came, they were just invited to come on in. This was an astounding phenomenon. It is doubtful if some of these people would have been reached if I had been in good health. When the people knew I wasn't able to carry on visitation, they came to visit us. This period was a growing one for the people of our church.

The invitation to go before the California congregation was not accepted until I, like Gideon, had put out a fleece. The Sedona church had accomplished many things in the way of acquiring furniture and equipment. All the needs of the building had been met. The problem was that we did not have enough space. If the church had been ready to build, I would have felt even more obligated to stay with them because of my building and money-raising experiences. Of course I did not tell anyone about this fleece. The church voted to delay building because the cost was so high. It hasn't been cheaper since.

I went before the church on the coast, telling them all I knew about my physical condition, but not expecting them to extend a call. They did! I asked for a week to make the decision. I've probably never walked and prayed more over anything. My wife, and our two children still at home, thought I was going to turn down the invitation. I had pretty well decided not to go. When the chairman of the pulpit committee called that Sunday afternoon, my mouth opened to say no, but it came out yes. I went.

Doris and our children stayed in Sedona until the end of the school year. I assumed the pastorate of the church in the San Diego area and began looking for a place to live. For the first time in my ministry we had to find our own residence. The congregation had previously sold their parsonage in order to permit their pastor to live where he wished. I did not like the idea at first, but we've never ceased being thankful that we were forced to buy property.

About a month or two later the daily paper ran a story on a new pain clinic in the Veterans Administration Hospital at La Jolla, Calif. Upon the recommendation of some of our members, I had already secured the service of a family doctor and did not go to this pain clinic for approximately six months. After I felt that my feet were somewhere near the ground in the new pastorate, I drove out to the VA Hospital to see what they would do for me.

Unless there is an emergency involved, one usually must wait at least a couple of weeks to be accepted as an inpatient by the VA. So it was quite a surprise when, after a screening examination, the doctor called the pain ward and told them he had a patient he thought would interest them. He explained the symptoms, listened for a moment, then asked, "Can you check in today?" I could and did.

They took me off Percodan gradually but kept up the Valium doses. It seems they threw everything they had at me during a four-week stay. There was counseling, self-hypnosis, biofeedback, special exercises, and so on. After recovering from the withdrawal effects of Percodan, I began to feel better; but after leaving the hospital, I was soon unable to function because of the return of all the pain. One thing I felt the doctors in the hospital failed to take into consideration was the amount of bed rest a patient received. Our family doctor renewed the Percodan medication along with the Valium.

After several months the leading neurosurgeon in the pain ward attended a medical convention. He was very favorably impressed with some experiments using electrical impulses to block pain impulses. Upon his return, he had an electrical engineer make a rather crude transcutaneous nerve stimulator. I was selected to be their first guinea pig. I was called in early one Monday morning but had to tell them I was to officiate at a funeral on Tuesday. "Fine," said the doctor. "We can have an on-the-job test."

I checked out Tuesday morning, in time for the service, wearing a box full of batteries and electrical parts on my belt. Two leads were taped to my back, under my clothing, and the electricity traveled through them and radiated across an area of the spine. I was able to give a good report on the experience. The doctor then had the hospital authorize Medtronics, Inc., to manufacture some more sophisticated ones. Probably I was the first patient, on the West Coast at least, to become a recipient of the new electrical gadget.

The leading theory of pain relief with the transcutaneous nerve stimulator, at least at that time, is known as the "gate" theory. This is based on the idea that only one

54

impulse can get through the "gate" of that portion of the brain at one time. The purpose of the T.N.S. is to send an electrical impulse through the gate and, at the same time, block out the pain impulses. (As a former farm boy, I conjured up a picture of separating hogs with a swinging gate. We did this when it was necessary to separate them for any reason. One person would hold the gate open just enough to let one hog through. Another person would be behind the hogs, encouraging them forward. Hogs are more aggressive than sheep or cattle. They all try to go through the gap at the same time. The person operating the gate has to be very careful, or they will crowd the gate open too far, and some of the wrong ones will get through. It is an exasperating task. In my mind's eye, I can see these little pain impulses and electrical impulses crowding to get through the "gate" and squealing like pigs.)

The stimulator worked well some of the time. There were problems, however. The electrodes had to be positioned upon the spine with great precision. My skin proved to be allergic to the tape that held the electrodes in place. I suffered so much pain that I would often leave it on at too high a level and burn myself. One time the burns were so bad that I could not tolerate the stimulator for at least a couple of months. At such time I would go back to Percodan or, if still taking some, increase the dosage.

Working long hours in the pastorate was difficult; the most pain came from the sitting position. A pastor usually sits while counseling, preparing sermons, driving, visiting in homes, attending meetings, and so on. Often when the obligations were apparently through for the day, Doris would meet me at the door, telling of some urgent need. With several pain pills in my mouth, I would be back in the car again. Life became a cycle of addiction, depression, inability to function well, hospitalization to withdraw me from addictive medication and provide some bed rest, and back on the job again. The hospital staff handled the addiction in various ways, from cold turkey to methadone. The methadone treatment felt, by far, the easiest.

There are many people who will sincerely declare that they will never resort to drugs under any circumstances. I well might have said that at an earlier date, but years of suffering have resulted in a low threshold of pain. The neurosurgeon who tried the experimental nerve stimulator often engaged in lively conversation regarding the nature of pain. The medical community, for the most part, admitted they knew little about the effects of pain on the individual, simply because they had not experienced pain to any extent. He had a very incomplete knowledge of it until his ankle was broken on a skiing trip. "I thought I would not be able to stand it until I was given a shot," he said. "It was the worst thing I have ever experienced."

"How long was it until you were given relief?" I asked. It was less than an hour, and because of the medication, he suffered no distress when the bone was set. He was able to have a convalescence relatively free from responsibility. My inward reaction was, "You still don't know what pain is."

There is very little real understanding. When one fights pain day after day, night after night, month after month, and year after year, one begins to know something about pain. I have not experienced the raging pain of some terminal cancer patients and, possibly, the extent of it in crippling arthritis, but I have lived with such pain that I felt it could no longer be endured. It's my belief that a person will do almost anything to ease himself when pain becomes severe enough. Often I prayed to die. I have considered suicide many times. It seemed so easy to collide with a concrete bridge support at high speed, or take an overdose of some of the very potent medication, or simply pull the trigger. Complicated planning filled nights when sleep would not come. But it seemed there were always certain things that would not fit together to save

56

my family and the church problems. Lest there be misunderstanding, I have never taken narcotics that the doctors have not prescribed. Also may we offer a bit of advice: Do not criticize the limp of another until you have walked a mile in his shoes. Don't be too adamant about what you would do or not do in any circumstance until you have actually experienced that circumstance.

After several years as both an inpatient and an outpatient of the pain ward, I reached certain conclusions. My pain was in no way psychosomatic; further surgery in the same area as the previous operations would be too dangerous; and I would have to live with what they had recommended. These were medication, the transcutaneous nerve stimulator, plenty of bed rest, water exercises, and whirlpool therapy when possible.

Subconsciously I knew that my body was demanding retirement. The thought of total disability at the age of 57 was very difficult to accept. Many are disabled much younger, and many are born with disabilities, but perhaps I thought I should receive an exemption because of the nature of my work.

5

God Cares for His Own

While lying in the hospital bed, I felt that it was hardly possible to continue the life we had known for the past 12 years. There was the realization that a certain plateau had been reached in my present pastorate. It wasn't one that indicated a move was in order, but certain goals had all been attained. The rather large church had been in deep trouble financially and in fellowship. The Lord used our period of service, even in my physical and emotional condition, to lead them out of their particular wilderness. There is no claim of credit for this; the Lord and His people had brought it to pass under my ministry. With the mortgage-burning service the church was completely out of debt and had over $12,000 in a savings account. There were some plans to use that, but they never came to fruition. A lady who had been a member of the church most of its existence, and was my first secretary, said, "This church doesn't know what to do with money because it has never had any."

The building that housed the sanctuary had been completely renovated. This included restyling the sanctuary with an arched front, a new rostrum and choir loft, new lighting, new P.A. system, wall-to-wall carpeting, new chancel furniture, new pews with spring seats and padded backs, new stained-glass windows, redecorated foyer and new outside front doors. The nursery in the educational building had been renovated, and the classrooms had been painted. The kitchen was furnished with new appliances and had received a new floor. The church had acquired new sound and visual equipment among other items. The parking lot was commercially asphalted, striped, and fenced.

Since all the goals had been reached, it seemed as if it might be time to resign and make room for a new leader. My prayers concentrated on what I should do. At the time of holding a match to the church mortgage I little thought this would be my last official act as pastor of the church. Yes, I had finally arrived at a decision. It was for disability. I would go for it!

Having made the decision to ask for disability status, I was amazed at how rapidly things happened. After being released from the hospital, I simply assembled my medical records beginning with the myelogram in 1966, plus a letter from the church and one from our family physician. The executive director of Metropolitan Missions was contacted to see if he had any advice. He had been very understanding and helpful during our years on the coast. As it happened, he was just ready to leave to attend the annual state convention meeting. He told me to write a cover letter for my records, that he would also write me a letter, and that he would collect them all and place them in the hands of the Annuity Board representative at the convention. This worked out quite well. A letter came from the board within a few days, stating that my request for disability had been approved, and I would begin receiving monthly checks in six months.

Past experience created misgivings about going to the Social Security Office to ask for help. As a pastor, I had dealt with several people who felt it was very difficult to be approved for disability. Dating from the days in the armed forces, it seemed that everything related to the government included "Hurry up and wait." Because of spinal problems, I could not sit for hours even if a comfortable chair could be found. I could just see myself stretched out on the floor and being in trouble for it.

The assistant pastor suggested he could call the Social Security Office and tell them his pastor needed an interview but was not able to sit and wait until someone could see him. He was just the man to do this. He was a very reasonable person and would never seem to become impatient when dealing with another. He invariably would find a common interest with another person, and this was to be no exception. The supervisor was an active Christian, although not of our particular persuasion. She graciously set up a date and time and told the associate to have me ask for her by name. When we arrived, she had an interviewer cleared and ready to help. "My best interviewer," she assured me as she helped me to a chair.

The interviewer, who was also very gracious, quickly surveyed the records, asked a few questions, and then said in effect, "I'll have to send this downtown to the Reviewing Board. After they approve it, they will send it to Baltimore. In the meantime, if you become anxious about anything, just phone me." I've never received more prompt, efficient, and polite treatment.

In a few days our doctor's office called. The Reviewing Board wanted some more information, and would I please come in? I went over immediately and found that the board wanted current measurements of my legs. The doctor was angry but I was amused. He thought they had more information than they needed and should know that anyone having constant pain wasn't able to work. He quickly took the required measurements. At that time the left leg was about two inches shorter and one and one-half inches smaller around than the right one.

Approximately two weeks passed. I decided to accept the interviewer's invitation and telephone her. "Everything is fine," she said. "The board approved your request and sent it on to Baltimore. You should hear any day now." Sure enough, we heard the next day. At most, it was a very brief wait. The payments were to begin in five months. With my request approved by our denomination's Annuity Board about a month previously, the first checks came just two days apart.

Whether anything can be done about the waiting period from time of approval for disability to the sending of the first check is debatable. Social Security has a five-month delay. The annuity board has six months. The wait is probably similar with other denominations' pension boards. This is a traumatic time for most applicants. It is a time when more money is required and less is available. One can only guess at some of the reasons for such a long delay, but from the experience of others, we know it can be a very difficult period.

The reaction of our congregation to the problem is cause for thanksgiving to God. The church could not pay me a salary during that time. Even if it had been permissible, I would have felt bad about taking it when I couldn't even attend services most of the time. In lieu of a salary they could and did give Doris a monthly gift of a check. They kept it from relating to my previous salary in any way. We could not keep our health insurance because it was on an associational group basis. We did not receive any of my allowances, just a gift that was enough to provide our living during that uncertain period. We shall never be able to thank them enough for taking care of us. How I wish every person who becomes disabled could have such wonderful, caring employers. Doris was right all along. All my worry was for nothing. The Lord would not let us starve! But He wasn't through yet!

My wife and I had occasionally discussed where and how we would live in retirement but had done little about it. We would not recommend our procedure to others, even though everything worked out well in our situation. We had considered renting a small apartment or possibly purchasing a used mobile home in good condition. Until the last pastorate, we had lived in a parsonage. In southern California we were forced to purchase a home. With the help of a real estate salesman, who eventually became a good friend, we found just what we wanted. It had three bedrooms, two baths, a double garage, and was perched on the first row of hills back from the Pacific. We could see the ocean from the back of the house, and the mountains from the front. It was as clean as a pin. It was owned by a career navy man and his Oriental wife, who was a remarkable housekeeper. Although the house was four years old, it looked like a new one. The husband was being transferred to the South Pacific and was taking his family with him. Doris and I conferred by phone about the house, and we bought it the day it was placed on multiple listing.

Sometime later we decided to sell the house and return to Missouri to be near relatives. When I checked the equity in our home, only about $1,600 had been paid on the principal. The rest of our payments had gone for interest and taxes. (I recalled at the time of purchase the figure 2002 on some papers. "What is that number?" I had inquired. "That is the year you will have completed your payment," came the answer. I had thought of 30 years of payments and of being 82 years of age. I knew I would never pay off the mortgage and had to consider the monthly payments as rent.) I phoned the agent who had sold us the house and told him we wanted to sell it. Since it had been purchased through him, we wanted to sell it through him.

The work of the church and my chronic pain had kept me too preoccupied to notice what had taken place in southern California real estate, but my agent made me aware of the escalation of property in our area. We wanted to sell the place for enough to buy a house back in Missouri. We had paid $25,000 for it in early 1972.

"How about taking back a $25,000 profit?" my friend asked.

"Why not ask $60,000 for this one rather than $50,000?" I countered.

"Good thinking," he said. "You can always lower your price, but once you have set one, you can't raise it." He then told me we should sell it ourselves and save the real estate commission. When I told him we knew nothing about selling a house, he promised to bring us a large "For Sale by Owner" sign, the necessary forms, and any instructions we would need. It worked out wonderfully well. The second prospect bought our $25,000 house for $59,950. We had not only no commission to pay but also no advertising expense. We sold it for 240 percent of our purchase price.

There was an interesting sidelight to this story as it touched the life of the real estate agent. During the purchase of the home and while the papers were still in escrow, this man entered the hospital for cancer surgery. The doctor's prognosis was that he would not survive the surgery.

Our church rallied in prayer for him, and I visited him each day. His employer had to finish the sale of the house to us, but he promised our agent would receive the commission. The man survived the cancer, and it's my belief it was one of God's miracles during those early days at the church. After that he became very active in the work of the American Cancer Society.

His church affiliation was with the Congregational church, but he had not attended regularly for a few years. I witnessed to him until he received the assurance of his salvation. He attended our worship services and looked upon me as his pastor, although he did not become a member of the church. Every time he would have a spiritual or personal problem, he would find his way to my study. As far as we know, he is still alive and well.

But getting back to the selling price of the house, I don't believe the Lord raised the price of real estate in all of southern California just so that we could make enough to buy a home in Missouri. However, I do believe He guided the situation, as far as we were concerned, from our buying the house to our selling it, and in this way provided us with a retirement home. Perhaps this was one of the things He had in mind when I opened my mouth to say no and said yes instead.

This is not advice to anyone to neglect the matter of retirement and a home, as we did. It is hardly fair to expect God to take care of all our own neglect. Nevertheless, we shall always call our house "God's house" because He provided it for us without our doing anything for it. In addition to making plans for a retirement home, I would also urge those who enter the ministry to begin participation immediately in whatever pension plan your denomination may have. Any delay may cost one in the amount of retirement benefits. If your plan has different levels of participation, choose the best one possible. I didn't. We thank the Lord for what we have but, if I had envisioned the need, I would have taken the more expensive. Also, don't permit anyone to talk, or scare, you away from Social Security participation. I believe Social Security will endure as long as our government does, or until Jesus returns. My wife and I could not survive without Social Security unless the Lord made other provisions for us.

Our church, although I had not been their pastor for several months, gave us a wonderful, surprise 40th wedding anniversary celebration. This was on May 1, 1978. I often tease Doris at such events by saying something like, "May Day used to be a pleasant day with children dancing around the Maypole, and so on. After we took it for our wedding day, it became an international distress signal."

When we moved back to Missouri, the church people loaded our rented moving van, saw that we had plenty to eat, and provided us with bed and breakfast before we left. Our youngest son married shortly before we moved, and they planned to make their home in Missouri also. He drove the van and pulled their car behind it. Doris and I drove one car and pulled another one. I was very ill at this time, so it was quite an ordeal.

If I had been in better health, we would have spent longer looking for our house in Missouri. But who knows? We might not have done as well. We had a list of ideas that we wished to follow, like a house not facing north; but in our hurry to get settled, we forgot all about it. You guessed it—we bought a house that faces north. However, we have been pleased with it and are so very thankful. It is a six-year-old house, on a relatively new cul-de-sac, in a small town four miles from our oldest son on one side and about seven miles from the church where I pastored nine and one-half years on the other. It is about 25 miles from downtown Kansas City. There are three bedrooms, one now used as my study; a dining room; a double garage; and a full basement. It had central heat, but some of the people we pastored years ago thought we should also have central air-conditioning. An air-conditioning man who had been our song leader years ago was able to get an excellent price for us, and he and a deacon of the church installed it. It has been such a blessing. I have to use a lot of heat on my back and legs. I don't know how I would do it in the summer without central air-conditioning.

In addition to our new home, we had enough profit left from our California house to purchase new kitchen and laundry appliances, a new dining room set, a new sofa bed for the living room, and a number of other things to set up house-keeping in a new place. Because of my affliction I need a special type of bed, chairs, and a heavy, easy-riding auto-mobile. We have been able to buy these things, including a new, large, luxury-type car. We could never have done these things without the graciousness of God and His people. After all this time there is still a family from the pastorate in Colo-rado who has continued to encourage and help us beyond all logical consideration. I like to believe that God has something very special awaiting them in His house of many mansions. I would not have bought such an expensive automobile as a pastor, even if I could have afforded it. Now, however, my body needs the easier ride provided by the extra weight of a large, trouble-free car.

In thinking of how the Lord has cared for us through the years, I recall an incident that happened at Sears. I gave the company a little more than a three-month notice of my leav-ing to enter the ministry. My intentions soon became known all over the plant. One day an acquaintance said, "Bill, I hate to see you leave the company, especially for the clergy. You will literally make a beggar of yourself. You will have to spend the rest of your life doing it."

"The Bride of Christ is no beggar," I replied, "and I don't believe God has called me to a life of begging to support my family."

Some of my plans must have appeared foolish to many people. They seemed so to members of both our families. I have never felt I should, or needed to, beg. I have never asked for a raise in salary. Indeed, I have refused several, feeling the church needed to build or carry out some other worthy pro-gram rather than just raise the pastor's salary. Much credit is due my wife. She has always been able to stretch a dollar and has not been one to make a lot of demands when we could not afford them. We have reared five children. I wish some of them might have felt God's call into full-time service and followed in their father's footsteps. None have. Possibly this has been my fault. It has not been easy to bear the burden of illness through the years. If they had never seen anything but victory in my life, it might have been different. Thank God they are all Christians. Furthermore, there isn't a single one of them afraid of work. In fact, all of them held jobs before they left home. They have also always been completely honest in their dealings with their parents and, I trust, with everyone else.

Not only has the Lord blessed our homelife in the area of finances, He has also blessed our churches. I have never begged for money in any church but have simply told the congregations what He expects of each one, showing them God's plan from His Word. I've tried to convince them by personal example, and they have done the rest. We have never left a pastorate when it was not financially sound and doing what should be done about giving to missions. Some might wonder if my affliction was caused as a punishment for failure to serve any of our flocks. I will not defend myself but will stand on the record in every church we've had the privilege to serve.

Well, we did "go for it!" I miss being a pastor. I can't think of anything I would really rather do. Yet, trying to carry on in my physical condition was virtually impossible. Taking this into consideration, I must say our life is better. It is better because the Lord has cared for us and provided so much more than we ever expected. I am in a constant state of thanksgiving, even when I'm in pain. Yes, yes, it is better. Praise His holy name!

6

Reasons and Responses

Pursuing the physical reasons for my condition, and failure to be physically victorious over it, caused me to feel like a detective trying to solve a case. There were blind alleys and dead ends, but there were more and more pieces of the puzzle coming together. Even in retirement I had not reached the end of the chase.

Soon after our return to Missouri, I visited the Veterans Administration Hospital in Kansas City. It did not have a pain clinic, and I had to become an outpatient in three other clinics to get the medications I had been receiving in California. Voluntarily, and with their permission, I cut back to two clinics. As I was having a checkup in the orthopedic clinic one day, the doctor was called from the examining room. I have never understood why a doctor does not want a patient to be familiar with his own medical records. It has been demonstrated that it helps most patients to be well informed. Yet, if the patient is asked to carry his records from one place to another, in a VA hospital, they are placed in a lock bag made for the purpose.

With my doctor out of the room, the chance had come. I began to peruse my records with as much haste as possible. Suddenly two words jumped out at me. SEVERE OSTEO-POROSIS! As I tried to decipher the records, it seemed that this was the reason the skeletal framework of my body was weak, failing to protect certain nerves adequately and causing much pain.

My prying was not discussed with the doctor when he returned, partly because I had been prying, and partly because he seemed to be in a hurry. If I had known it was the last time we would be together I would have insisted that he explain the problem a bit more. The diagnosis, as I was able to comprehend it, seemed logical. Shortly afterward I had major abdominal surgery and, while convalescing, asked an intern about osteoporosis. "That's a woman's disease," he answered quickly and didn't seem to want to talk about it. Frankly, from his definition and reluctance to discuss it, I concluded he did not know much about it.

After being able to resume outpatient status and having kept the first postoperative appointment with the orthopedic clinic, I was assigned to another doctor. He had checked my record and said that all he could really do was prescribe the medication. He said that if I approved, he would place me in an outpatient medical group, and most of the time, I could just come and pick up the medication without having to see him. It sounded good. However, when I arrived at the medical group area, the first question was, "Can you afford to pay for this medicine yourself?" I answered, "Yes," so she suggested having our family physician prescribe it.

We had not acquired the services of a family doctor at the time, but there seemed to be no reason to discuss it. It was far more expensive, however, than just paying for the medicine. Our new doctor required an appointment every two weeks for a few months. My status now is that the doctor must approve the pain prescription each time it is filled, but I make only an occasional office call, and that at his request.

We wanted to purchase an adjustable power bed for my use, and desired a doctor's prescription for tax purposes. Doris obtained the form while making an office call for herself. When I looked at the form, my eyes quickly picked out two questions and the doctor's answers to them. They were:

> Diagnosis? Osteoporosis.
> Prognosis? Guarded

There was no mention of the back problem nor of the pain that was so constantly with me. There had been absolutely no contact between our new doctor and the VA Hospital on this case. I had never mentioned the diagnosis on the VA file. Yet he had come to the same conclusion. Osteoporosis was worthy of further investigation. It is true that a larger percentage of older women are afflicted with it than are older men. However, it is not just "a woman's disease." For years my doctors had talked in terms of degenerative disease, deterioration of both bones and disks, soft bones, and, perhaps not so jokingly, my need of a spinal transplant. The doctor could not tell me much about it, but the following is taken from *The American Medical Association Family Medical Guide.* (Random House, 543, italics added):

> Osteoporosis is the wasting, or deterioration, of bone. In healthy bone, there is a balance between the breakdown of the old bone tissue and the manufacture of new, replacement material. In osteoporosis, breakdown occurs faster than replacement, and the bones become *soft* and *weak*.
>
> Osteoporosis may occur in one or more bones after prolonged immobilization of part of the body, possibly because of a fracture or *prolapsed disc*. Some hormonal disorders may cause some osteoporosis. It may

also result from a *diet low in protein and calcium,* which are needed to maintain healthy bones. . . .

Osteoporosis does not usually produce symptoms unless it occurs in the *vertebrae,* or backbone. . . .

Professional help: There is no specific treatment for osteoporosis. Your physician may prescribe calcium tablets to slow down the wasting process.

It seems the pieces of the puzzle have come together and have made a complete picture. Deficiency of calcium from a baby, rachitis as a child, the seeming inability to have broken bones as a youth, the soft and porous bone condition discovered in surgery, the inability of my skeletal frame to prevent pressure on nerves, and the failure of bone fusions to stabilize my back, although a full body cast did. It is easier to understand the relief experienced when I submerge my body in water. To give that relief, the water must be around shoulder depth. I can stand in this depth, usually without pain, because my body becomes relatively weightless. The buoyance of the water becomes roughly equal to the pull of gravity. The problem is that when I ascend the steps out of the pool, the weight of my body settles, and the pain and numbness returns.

When one is young and has a calcium deficiency, the bones are soft in that they will bend and often prevent a fracture. After one is elderly, the bones are soft in one sense of the word. Actually, they are porous and have lost a certain amount of bone mass. They become easily broken, and the person having osteoporosis should take great care to prevent falls or anything that would place unusual pressure on his bones.

My life has been full of ups and downs. One day I was a schedule boss at Sears; the next day I was a private in the armed forces and wasn't telling anyone what to do. One day I was a buyer at Sears, being trained for promotion; the next day I was a college freshman, a church janitor, and an honor-

MARVIN by Tom Armstrong
© by and permission of
News America Syndicate, 1986.

ary assistant pastor. (The word *honorary* was added because the church could scratch up enough money to pay for some janitor work, but they couldn't afford another paid staff member.) One day I had my college and seminary training, and a few years as a successful pastor; new opportunities for service were developing. The next day I was flat on my back with a heart attack that affected my health for years. Another day I had seemed to have regained my health and was enjoying more years in the pastorate; doors for denominational work were opening. The next day I was down with a permanent spinal injury. Again I endured two pastorates that would have been a delight without my affliction; then total and permanent disability. If the sudden stops in my life had not hurt so much, I would characterize my lifework as a yo-yo.

Having reached this stage of life, I've come to believe that one's responses to physical problems are more important than the reasons for them. "In all this Job sinned not, nor charged God foolishly" (Job 1:22). I no longer feel any bitterness about my situation. I would be exceedingly foolish if, even in my heart, I were in any way to blame God. No longer do I feel He owes me an explanation, but I do owe Him my trust. It is not explanations but continued revelations, that I need. When first entering the ministry, I would not have been surprised at hunger stalking our paths, nor would I have been perturbed had it been necessary for me to supplement our income with secular work. I was determined to begin on faith, and I have never earned a dime outside the church since leaving secular work. That is not a boast, just the fact that God takes care of His own. Paul wrote the Philippians, "My God shall supply all your need according to his riches in glory by Christ Jesus" (4:19). Jesus said, in the Sermon on the Mount, "Your Father knoweth what things ye have need of, before ye ask him" (Matt. 6:8). Again in the same chapter He said, "Seek ye first the kingdom of God, and his righteousness; and all these things shall be added unto you" (v. 33).

Many pastors have endured serious disagreements with their congregations. Indeed, some have been forced to resign. There are different kinds of pain we sometimes have to bear. I would not be able to stand the pain of dissension for very long. I am not noble in that way. My pain has been physical. The Lord comes to the rescue of all who suffer pain of any kind. Paul wrote, "There hath no temptation taken you but such as is common to man: but God is faithful, who will not suffer you to be tempted above that ye are able; but will with the temptation also make a way to escape, that ye may be able to bear it" (1 Cor. 10:13). Some of our own churches have experienced divisions, either before we came, or sometime after we left, but not while we traveled along with them. I cannot think of any of our flocks without love and gratitude. Yes, more love for some than for others; this is inherent in our humanity. But how I would like to tell all of them how I love and appreciate them. I'm sure I did far too little of it when we were with them.

The Lord sees to it that our needs are well met. We have five children, 10 grandchildren, and one great-grandchild, all healthy. My wife is very involved in the program of our local church. I attend the Sunday morning worship services when physically able. We have a fine pastor. Sometimes I am able to preach for him. I have written a number of articles on stewardship and on building programs for the church. We now have a new building. I have taught the Sunday School lessons on cassette tapes for the homebound. Of course, we support the church financially. I had hoped, during retirement, to preach revivals, do supply and interim work, teach church studies, and so on. Thus far, things simply have not worked out that way. I see no help for it but a miracle. In the meantime, I will do what I can.

It is often amusing that some people feel I need something to do. Some actively seek out projects for me. It is true I cannot do many things I would like, but there is no problem keeping busy. We have a branch of the 36th-largest public library system in the nation, just a block away. So there is access to many books. Although it requires a bit more pain medication, I try to get out for shopping and lunch at least once a week with Doris. Time passes rapidly, and there are still many things I can do for which time has not yet been found. I may not know all the reasons for the health problems, although most of the physical ones are now clear, but may my responses for the Lord's care always be filled with gratitude. If there are other reasons, I shall know them when standing before Him.

7

The Struggle with
Responsibility

One of the most difficult tasks of the conscientious seeker is trying to place responsibility for the happenings in this world. It is said that Benjamin Franklin was a Deist. The doctrine of Deism is usually defined as the belief in a Supreme Being as the Source of finite existence, but to the exclusion of revelation and the supernatural doctrines of Christianity. One might illustrate Deism by comparing it to a clockmaker who made a clock, wound it up, and, touching it no more, let it run down. This is the belief that God made His creation to be controlled by certain rules, such as the law of gravitation, and then ceased to intervene in its history. Man should seek to discover these laws and live in harmony with them. When nature goes on a rampage, it is simply the cumulative results of the interaction of these laws. When man doesn't play by the rules, he will find himself in trouble, and it is useless to believe there is a personal God who will come to his aid.

Probably the other side of this coin is that God involves himself in everything that happens. On the surface this sounds good. We definitely believe in prayer, both praying for others and praying for ourselves. Prayer certainly does change things and will doutlessly change us. My simple faith is much like the little girl's who was taking a safety test in her class at school. One of the questions was, "Who is responsible to see you safely across the street?" Without hesitation she wrote, "God"! When grading the papers, the teacher saw it was not the expected answer, but she had to smile through a tear and a lump in her throat anyway.

Perhaps the questions about to be raised may seem less sacrilegious to some who know my faith. Does God use tidal waves to drown thousands of men, women, and children indiscriminately? Does He reach down and shake the earth so that thousands are squashed beneath the rubble of their homes, without regard to their faith or life-style? Does He cause a hurricane to kill a few selected people and destroy the property of all the others within a given area? Will He lift a tornado over my house and deliberately drop it on my neighbor's home, killing all his children? Does He twist the steering wheel of a speeding truck, causing it to cross the median and smash headon into a car full of children on their way to a religious encampment? Is this the way God punishes and rewards us? Or is He a capricious sadist who delights himself in the misery of His victims?

There is some truth to be found in both of these viewpoints, but it should be handled with extreme care. No doubt God has created certain functioning laws to control His universe. The more we discover about them and use them in the right way, the better the state of man will be. However, a Christian cannot be a Deist. The two are contradictory. The

Incarnation is the best example of God's interventions in human history.

On the other hand, we find that God has treated groups of people harshly at times. Plenty of evidence is recorded in the Old Testament. We also find He gave ample warning and an opportunity for people to change the direction of their lives. His punishment was never capricious nor unjust, but consistent and fair. Consider the pagan city of Nineveh for an example. He warned them of destruction through the preaching of Jonah. He had sent Jonah to warn them, and it was not His fault that Jonah at first resisted his assignment. In spite of Jonah's belated efforts, the people repented and God saved them. The messages of the prophets were, with great consistency, calls to repentance and obedience. We must not forget that God was trying to develop a nation of priests at the crossroads of humanity. Few of the Hebrews understood the evangelistic heart of God. We often say that the end does not justify the means. I feel this is almost always true. Perhaps we could sanction an exception when we realize God's end was always to save all people. He is "not willing that any should perish, but that all should come to repentance" (2 Pet. 3:9).

Just about the time one is convinced that the order is sin, followed by punishment, God places an example to the contrary right in the middle of the Old Testament—the story of Job. Here was a man perfect and upright, one that feared God and hated evil. (See Job 1:1.) Nobody deserved to escape suffering as much as Job, yet nobody, at that time, suffered more. Job proved he had not followed God just because of what God had given him. He continued to follow the Giver after the gifts had been taken away. Job was the best example of faithfulness to God at that time, but it seemed from his human vantage point that God failed to be faithful to him. He faithfully clung to God when his wife urged him to curse Him and die. He kept trusting in God's justice when he felt he had grounds to think Him unjust.

The New Testament ushered in a certain mellowing of divine dealings with people. Jesus warned of judgment in the ages to come, but the people who suffered most in the first century were His own followers. Other people, especially the Jews, brought persecution upon them. I cannot remember a single miracle Jesus performed to punish anyone. There were times when He seemed reluctant that anyone be told of His miracles. In fact, He sometimes asked His disciples to be quiet about them. His only times of anger were when He drove the money changers from the Temple grounds and on other occasions rebuked the hypocritical Pharisees. Yet, with all His gentleness, He was very intense and exceedingly strong of character.

When we turn to the Bible to seek responsibility for suffering, we may find some surprises. One day as Jesus was teaching in a synagogue on the Sabbath, He saw a crippled woman and healed her. The ruler of the synagogue criticized Him since healing was considered labor. Jesus answered, "Ought not this woman, being a daughter of Abraham, whom Satan hath bound, lo, these eighteen years, be loosed from this bond on the sabbath day?" (Luke 13:16). Here Jesus clearly blamed Satan for the woman's condition. This compares favorably with Job's plight. Although God allowed it, Satan afflicted Job with all his misfortune. It may surprise some that the source of Paul's "thorn in the flesh" was Satan. One of Paul's letters to the church at Corinth states, "And lest I should be exalted above measure through the abundance of the revelations, there was given to me a thorn in the flesh, the messenger of Satan to buffet me" (2 Cor. 12:7). You will recall Paul prayed for healing three times, but God told him His grace was sufficient for him (see verses 8-10). Satan is active in the world. In 1 Pet. 5:8 we read, "Be sober, be vigilant; because your adversary the devil, as a roaring lion, walketh about, seeking whom he may devour." Jesus, Paul, and James had much to say about Satan. Many life-styles and bad habits, encouraged by the devil, are the cause of much suffering and death today. James wrote, "Resist the devil, and he will flee from you" (4:7). We certainly need more of our people to resist the devil in our day.

There is a strange experience, already mentioned briefly, in John 9. "And as Jesus passed by, he saw a man which was blind from his birth. And his disciples asked him, saying, Master, who did sin, this man, or his parents, that he was born blind? Jesus answered, Neither hath this man sinned, nor his parents: but that the works of God should be made manifest in him" (vv. 1-3). One must accept the fact that neither the blind man nor his parents were in any way responsible for the man's affliction. As you read the entire chapter, you will find that Jesus restored the man's sight. The amazing thing is that the afflicted man did not know the identity of Jesus when He healed him. Near the end of the chapter it is recorded that Jesus and the man met again. This time Jesus told him who He was, and the man believed in Him. Who was responsible for the man's blindness?

There is a similarity in this event to the death of Lazarus. In John 11:1, 3-4, we read, "Now a certain man was sick, named Lazarus, of Bethany, the town of Mary and her sister Martha. . . . Therefore his sisters sent unto him, saying, Lord, behold, he whom thou lovest is sick. When Jesus heard that, he said, This sickness is not unto death, but for the glory of God, that the Son of God might be glorified thereby." Later in the chapter, the story says Lazarus died and Jesus raised him from the dead. The point is that Lazarus' sickness and the man's blindness in the previous paragraph were for essentially the same purpose. But who was responsible for Lazarus' sickness? If we were to say that God was responsible for both, then I must add that four days was not very long in Lazarus' life, but being blind from birth was a mighty long time in the blind man's life just so he could be healed as evidence of God's power. The city was full of blind men who could have been used.

In Luke 13:1-3 we read, "There were present at that season some that told him of the Galilaens, whose blood Pilate had mingled with their sacrifices. And Jesus answering said unto them, Suppose ye that these Galilaeans were sinners above all the Galilaeans, because they suffered such things? I tell you, Nay: but, except ye repent, ye shall all likewise perish." Jesus said these Galileans, who were slain by Pilate's order, were no more sinful than any other Galileans. Who was responsible for their deaths? Perhaps these fellows were just unfortunate enough to be selected for sacrifice by chance, out of a larger group. Some blame certainly must be placed at Pilate's door. Verse 4 reads, "Or those eighteen, upon whom the tower in Siloam fell, and slew them, think ye that they were sinners above all men that dwelt in Jerusalem?" Again Jesus said that those 18 victims were no more sinful than any of the men of Jerusalem. Again I ask, who was responsible? Maybe the legs of the tower were rotted and weak, and the tower collapsed as an accident. Or maybe a stray gust of wind hit the tower just right to tumble it over on the 18 citizens who had picked the wrong time to be there. Does the Bible rule out all accidents?

Jesus' mission was not primarily a crusade against disease. He defined His ministry in His hometown, from the Book of Isaiah, as cited in Luke 4:18-19: "The Spirit of the Lord is upon me, because he hath anointed me to preach the gospel to the poor; he hath sent me to heal the brokenhearted, to preach deliverance to the captives, and recovering of sight to the blind, to set at liberty them that are bruised, to preach the acceptable year of the Lord." The restoration of sight to the blind is mentioned; but it seems that in most translations the preaching of the gospel, or the Good News, receives precedence over all else. If healing had been a high priority, surely our Lord would not have left so many unhealed.

There are several examples, but John 5:2-9 is one of the clearest. "Now there is at Jerusalem by the sheep market a pool, which is called in the Hebrew tongue Bethesda, having five porches. In these lay a great multitude of impotent folk, of blind, halt, withered, waiting for the moving of the water. For an angel went down at a certain season into the pool, and troubled the water: whosoever then first after the troubling of the water stepped in was made whole of whatsoever disease he had. And a certain man was there, which had an infirmity thirty and eight years. When Jesus saw him lie, and knew that he had been now a long time in that case, he saith unto him, Wilt thou be made whole? The impotent man answered him, Sir, I have no man, when the water is troubled, to put me into the pool: but while I am coming, another steppeth down before me. Jesus saith unto him, Rise, take up thy bed, and walk. And immediately the man was made whole, and took up his bed, and walked." There was a great multitude of sick people there, but Jesus healed only one. His ministry included work with many individuals, some of whom had a disease. You may be thinking that only this man had enough faith, or that maybe he was the only one willing to follow Jesus. But as you read more of the chapter, you will find the healed man didn't even know the identity of Jesus. Later Christ made contact with him and told him, "Behold, thou art made whole: sin no more, lest a worse thing come unto thee" (v. 14). The man showed his gratitude by going directly to the Jews, who wanted to kill Jesus, and telling them who He was. I'm not at all sure he knew any more about Jesus than His name even after this second contact with Him.

It is difficult to establish a pattern in the New Testament. One man was healed at the Pool of Bethesda; a multitude of others were not. Paul was used to heal others, yet his own request for healing was denied. Peter was freed from prison; John the Baptist was executed. The widow who lived in Nain was blessed by the raising of her son; many other sons died and stayed dead. We could go on and on. From the evidence, it seems we should not become too self-satisfied with any one idea of who is responsible for suffering or what the qualifications are to be healed.

As far as the responsibility for afflictions is concerned, we seem to have placed some of it on Satan, none of it on Jesus, some of it possibly by accident, some of it on ourselves, and much of it on other people.

We have mentioned something of God's actions in the Old Testament. If you will make a study of such actions, you will find that God afflicted so many individuals and groups that it would take an entire book to deal with all of them. As previously stated, God was fair. He gave warning, and He punished for sin and disobedience. To Israel in the wilderness, God compared himself as a father to a son. "Thou shalt also consider in thine heart, that, as a man chasteneth his son, so the Lord thy God chasteneth thee" (Deut. 8:5). In Heb. 12:7-8 there is a related passage, "If ye endure chastening, God dealeth with you as with sons; for what son is he whom the father chasteneth not? But if ye be without chastisement, whereof all are partakers, then are ye bastards, and not sons." Lam. 1:12 offers a clear example: "Is it nothing to you, all ye that pass by? behold, and see if there be any sorrow like unto my sorrow, which is done unto me, wherewith the Lord hath afflicted me in the day of his fierce anger." In the Old Testament, as in the New Testament, one finds complaints about persecution by others. In Ps. 143:3 David complains, "For the enemy hath persecuted my soul; he hath smitten my life down to the ground; he hath made me to dwell in darkness, as those that have been long dead." David did a lot of complaining about his treatment at the hands of others.

We've said little about the monster of self where responsibility is concerned. It is rather easy to confuse self and Satan. "The devil made me do it" is a partly joking, partly serious response sometimes. People often know they are at fault. Honesty might require us to say, "I'm sick because of my poor diet, or little proper exercise, or overindulgence, or not keeping the rules, or not following medical advice."

I know I must accept much responsibility for my own health problems. Fairness would seem to excuse me from blame for a calcium deficiency as a baby and a small child. However, I have been very selective and stubborn about my diet most of my life. I've wanted to eat only what I've wanted, and I've wanted all the wrong things.

It was said I was a headstrong child and youth. Perhaps weak-minded would have been a better description. I felt everything that moved should move fast, especially horses and cars. A neighbor once asked my parents if I would ride my horse more slowly to and from school. They were afraid for their daughter's safety because her horse tried to keep up with mine. My egotistical answer was, "I haven't asked her to ride with me. When I start for home, I'm going home, and she can go where she pleases."

By the age of 10 I was driving cars. That sounds almost incredible today. But first, there were no driving licenses then. Second, I was working on the farm with the men at the age of 10. Third, my father didn't like to drive, and my mother never learned. I had a few minor accidents, such as sliding off the road when turning a corner too fast, before I really rolled one, as mentioned in an earlier chapter, at age 16. Alcohol and speed were the reasons for the latter. Driving while intoxicated (DWI) is a serious offense today, as it should be. I wonder what I would have done if I had been faced with the drug problem that now preys on our children and youth.

I'm not blaming anyone, but both smoking and drinking came rather naturally. My father farmed extensively until the middle of my first year in high school. We always had several farmhands. Almost all of them drank and smoked, including my father and brother. I stopped drinking when I married, and smoking when I met Christ.

If my spinal problems didn't start at 16, they certainly did at 19. The story was told in the chapter "From Birth to Rebirth," but the real cause was pride! At 16 I was proud to be the fastest driver and have the fastest car in town, a 1934 Ford V-8. I rather enjoyed the image of "tough guy" promoted by tobacco and alcohol. At 19 my pride was hurt because I had to work on the WPA. Nobody was going to call me lazy because of it.

Now, before you start feeling too pious about yourself, did you know that Jesus used His strongest language to denounce the twin sins of piousness and pride? Jesus had to deal with them constantly. One sees overtones of them in so many of His parables. His disciples consistently stumbled at these two points. They were more concerned about who was the greatest among them, and who would have the highest place of honor in heaven, than they were about fishing for men. Jesus spoke often to them about humility and self-sacrifice. He even called little children out of the crowds to illustrate the attitude people must have in order to enter into the kingdom of heaven. There could be no puffed-up piousness or stiff-necked pride, just the simple response and willingness of a little child. Humility played its part in His washing the disciples' feet, although I don't believe it was the main lesson. The lessons didn't really register with the disciples until after the Crucifixion, possibly not until after Pentecost. Pride and false piousness are terrible sins because they are completely contrary to the spirit of Christianity.

There is no doubt I am responsible for my problems in other ways, but the last to be dealt with here is not playing by the rules. I always tried to be back on the job in the shortest possible time after any illness. It might have appeared differently after the spinal surgeries, but they were still extremely painful when I returned to full service. I did not understand the condition of my bones, but I did know I hurt too much to be on the job. You see, believe it or not, pain is a gift of God. It is a marvelously designed alarm and protective system. If you touch a red-hot stove, what happens? Your pain sensors race to your brain with an order to remove the affected part. One doesn't stop and think whether or not one wants to remove his hand. One doesn't consider arguments on either side of the question. One doesn't have to think. No conscious decision is required. One just does it! Well, my pain sensors have sent millions of messages saying in effect, "Get off your feet! Lie down! Submerge your body in water!" I should have been an astronaut. Maybe I could have found a way to stay out of the pull of gravity most of the time. Instead of listening to the commands of my pain sensors, I have taken more pain tablets or turned up my electronic nerve stimulator, or both. I have overridden God's built-in alarm system. I haven't played by the rules, and I'm paying for it every day. As I struggle with the placement of responsibility, I can't shrug off my own involvement. I must place a considerable amount of the blame on myself. In Gal. 6:7 Paul wrote, "For whatsoever a man soweth, that shall he also reap."

8

God Took His Own Medicine

There was a time, I must admit, when I felt some bitterness toward God. How could I stand before others and convince them of God's love when they knew I hurt so badly? How could I deal with the great healing passages in the Bible when I had not been healed? How could I visit the sick and pray for their healing when I wanted to tell them to give me their sickbed because, at least in some instances, I needed it worse than they? How could I expect prospects to come to a church where the pastor was obviously ill and probably could not care for them as a pastor should? So many tormenting thoughts added to my feelings of frustration and made my affliction seem even worse.

One day a prospect almost stunned me with his words: "I could never worship a God who would let His own Son be murdered in such a barbaric manner. I don't believe in a bloody religion."

It startled and shamed me to realize I had entertained similar thoughts about God's failure to relieve me, one of His ministers, from the pain that made His work so difficult. Although I had often said that God did not need anyone to defend Him, that is exactly what I began to do.

"I don't believe you have all the facts," I told the young gentleman. "You see, Jesus said, 'I and my Father are one' (John 10:30). John also wrote, 'In the beginning was the Word, and the Word was with God, and the Word was God. . . . And the Word was made flesh, and dwelt among us' (1:1, 14). Just the evening before He died, Jesus said to one of His disciples, 'Have I been so long time with you, and yet hast thou not known me, Philip? he that hath seen me hath seen the Father; and how sayest thou then, Shew us the Father?' (14:9)."

I wish I could have read him the following paragraph from *Christian Letters to a Post-Christian World,* by Dorothy L. Sayers:

> For whatever reason God chose to make man as he is—limited and suffering and subject to sorrows and death—He had the honesty and courage to take His own medicine. Whatever game He is playing with His creation, He has kept His own rules and played fair. He can exact nothing from man that He has not exacted from Himself. He has Himself gone through the whole of human experience, from the trivial irritations of family life and the cramping restrictions of hard work and lack of money to the worst horrors of pain and humiliation, defeat, despair, and death. When He was a man, He played the man. He was born in poverty and died in disgrace and thought it well worthwhile.

We must insist that God did not make man as he is today. He created him without sin. He placed him in a garden and took care of all his needs. The important aspect is how Ms. Sayers expressed Christ's incarnation, and His suffering even the minute details of living a human life.

Christ was the only one in history who could plan His own birth. As Paul wrote, He "made himself of no reputation, and took upon him the form of a servant, and was made in the likeness of men: and being found in fashion as a man, he humbled himself, and became obedient unto death, even the death of the cross" (Phil. 2:7-8). *He* did it!

He was born of a poor mother, and a manger was His first crib. Probably a stone manger, as I discovered on a visit to Bethlehem. He suffered the discomfort of a flight to Egypt to escape the death edict of King Herod. I visited a cellarlike structure in Nazareth, said to be His childhood home. True or not, His childhood was far from affluent. Even the town of Nazareth was despised, and it seems the people might not have been too particular or proud. Yet its citizens, Jesus' own neighbors, chased Him from the synagogue and tried to kill Him. He did not make a handsome man of himself, in spite of all the pictures we have to the contrary. Isa. 53:2 states, "There is no beauty that we should desire him." His followers were mainly laborers who seemed to be pretty low on the economic scale. He experienced short periods of popularity, but His ministry was marked by persecution.

The events surrounding His death were gruesome. He was dragged from trial to trial. They struck Him and spat upon Him. They ridiculed the idea of His being their King in that they placed a crown of thorns upon His head and a purple robe about Him. I doubt that we can imagine the pain and thirst of the Crucifixion. The cross was one of the cruelest instruments of death man ever invented. Rome would not allow a Roman citizen to be crucified. The apostle Paul, for instance, although his death was eagerly sought, could not have been crucified because he was born free. The cross was reserved for slaves and foreigners. The Jews usually stoned criminals to death, but they never used crucifixion. This seems to make the blame even greater for those Jews who shouted, "Crucify him, crucify him" (Luke 23:21; John

88

19:6). There can be no doubt it brought the most extreme anguish and suffering, and it was also a death of the greatest dishonor.

Now you may think it sacrilegious of me, but as terrible as the shame and physical pain of the Crucifixion, it lasted only a few hours. As a pastor, I have watched members of my flock suffer terribly for days, and weeks, and even years. I have walked through large charity wards where the destitute on every side were moaning and screaming with the raging pain of terminal cancer, or some other dreadful disease. I have seen veterans suffering agonies that began on the battlefields and ended only in death. I have suffered for over 20 years myself, and often a doctor's most comforting words have been, "You must learn to live with it." There have been many times I would rather have died with it. Many think there will always be medication to stop one's pain in this modern day. This may have some truth in it for a short-term illness, but the medical profession will not allow the quantity needed for long-term chronic pain. Enough of the kind of medication to kill all my pain over the last 20 years would probably have killed me quite some time ago. Well then, although it will not compare with our capital punishment methods of today, when we try to make the criminal's death as comfortable as possible, what's the big deal about dying on a cross? Many did in Jesus' day. But here is how Jesus' death was different from all others in the history of mankind.

There is a song, a favorite of mine, which musically states, "No One Ever Cared for Me like Jesus." No one ever hurt for me, and for all mankind, like Jesus either! I don't wish to seem to mitigate the agony of the rough spikes driven through His hands and feet, nor the anguish of their tearing jerk when His cross was dropped into the hole prepared for it, but there was much more to His death than the physical pain. He did not react as others. No evil word, nor entreaty for mercy, passed His lips. Instead, He prayed for His tormentors. Perhaps He prayed for all mankind who "know not what they do" (Luke 23:34), rather than just the Roman soldiers who nailed Him to His cross. The Jews in high places, the rabble who always collect on such occasions, and even the passersby derided Him. He could have come down from the Cross. He could have called legions of angels to His aid. The crowd's contemptuousness must have been extremely frustrating when He knew He could stop dying for them at any time. However, He could not stop it and still bear the sin of the world.

Surely here we begin to touch upon His greatest anguish. He occupied himself during the first three hours (9 A.M. to 12 noon) with prayer, saving the soul of a thief, and committing His mother to John's care. Suddenly, at high noon, the brilliant Syrian sun hid its face, and darkness was over the land from 12 to 3 P.M. This surely was a time of the greatest anguish of spirit and physical pain. His sense of isolation and loneliness must have increased. Near the close of the period of darkness, and piercing through what must now have been an uneasy stillness, rang Jesus' words that have echoed down through the centuries: "Eloi, Eloi, lama sabachthani?" Translated from Aramaic, they are, "My God, my God, why hast thou forsaken me?" (Mark 15:34; cf. Matt. 27:46).

I will not pretend I know all that was involved in Jesus' cry. Perhaps what I do believe may seem ambiguous. We have previously made it plain that Jesus was God in human flesh. Christ bore the sin of the world. In fact, He became sin. In 2 Cor. 5:21 Paul wrote, "For he hath made him to be sin for us, who knew no sin." Now God cannot look upon sin. Somehow, during this period, be it the full time or only a split second, the fellowship was broken. Divinity turned away from what had become sin. Jesus, who knew no sin, took upon himself total sin. His overwhelming grief and suffering, even greater than that in the Garden, when great drops of

90

blood gathered upon His forehead, crushed the bitter and desolate cry from His lips. It was the only time He cried out from His sufferings. There is no way, and there are no words, to convey the extent of His pain. It exceeded any physical pain by so much that there is no basis for comparison.

The same may be said of His love. The greatest love, both in quality and quantity, was centered there on that rugged Cross. I've often preached that it was His love for man, and not the nails, that held Him on the Cross. Yes, Jesus suffered more, and cared more, than any person who has ever inhabited this earth, or who ever will. In spite of the nature of Jesus' cry, He could not have been more pleasing to the Father. He was doing exactly what He came to do. Within moments He said, "It is finished" (John 19:30). I believe this was a triumphant cry. Then He bowed His head and said, "Father, into thy hands I commend my spirit" (Luke 23:46). Defeated? No! Victorious! Victory over death and sin and Satan! Only through Him may we taste of that victory.

There are two definite benefits we have realized from the death of Jesus. The first, of course, is that Jesus died for our sin, and we may have eternal life because of our faith in Him. The second is that we are never alone in our suffering because we have a living Savior who has suffered to the uttermost.

I once stood in the Garden Tomb and gave thanks that Jesus was not there but had risen. I was thinking of going to be with Him in heaven then. Now I realize He knows all about my pain. Even in the darkest hours of the night, when pain often seems the worst, I know He will not leave me nor forsake me (see Heb. 13:5). Not only will I not have to "cross Jordan" alone, but also I don't have to endure my pain alone. Yes, God took His own medicine and drained the cup of every dreg!

9

Though He Slay Me

Although the Lord may not choose to heal me in this life for His own reasons, I will be perfectly healed when I go to be with Him. This I know. Hallelujah! It is just a matter of time! And what is earth time compared with eternity? And what is affliction of the flesh compared with heavenly glory? Paul wrote the church at Corinth, "For our *light affliction,* which is *but for a moment,* worketh for us *a far more exceeding and eternal weight of glory*" (2 Cor. 4:17, italics mine).

I have suffered little real persecution for the cause of Christ, but perhaps it may be said I have suffered affliction because of persisting in doing His work while in severe pain. Suffering, of itself, does not automatically lead to glory. It brings glory only when it is done for the Lord. I admit, for the sake of my own physical health, I have been very foolish at times. Yet cannot perseverance in adverse circumstances be counted as a test, or trial, of one's faith? In 1 Pet. 1:4-7 we read that we have been born again "to an inheritance incorruptible, and undefiled, and that fadeth not away, reserved in heaven for you, who are kept by the power of God through faith unto salvation ready to be revealed in the last time. Wherein ye greatly rejoice, though now for a season, if need be, ye are in heaviness through manifold temptations: that the trial of your faith, being much more precious than of gold that perisheth, though it be tried with fire, might be found unto praise and honour and glory at the appearing of Jesus Christ."

It seems we have been given certain promises of benefits that accrue from personal affliction. For instance, Paul wrote the church at Rome, "And not only so, but we glory in tribulations also: knowing that tribulation worketh patience; and patience, experience; and experience, hope: and hope maketh not ashamed; because the love of God is shed abroad in our hearts by the Holy Ghost which is given unto us" (5:3-5). James took a similar position when he wrote, "My brethren, count it all joy when ye fall into divers temptations; knowing this, that the trying of your faith worketh patience. But let patience have her perfect work, that ye may be perfect and entire, wanting nothing" (1:2-4). I still find encouragement and often joy, in Rom. 8:28: "And we know that all things work together for good to them that love God, to them who are the called according to his purpose." The writer of Hebrews tells us that even Jesus learned obedience through suffering. He writes, "Though he were a Son, yet learned he obedience by the things which he suffered" (5:8).

The New Testament offers little encouragement to people to become Christians and then expect to suffer less because of it. In fact, just the opposite is true. The Books of Hebrews, James, and 1 Peter warn over and over that Christians will suffer. Paul suffered much and did not hesitate to reveal it. However, his writings are full of the joy and glory that will be ours when we go to spend eternity with Jesus. I have stood at the head of many open graves and read 1 Cor. 15:50-58:

> Now this I say, brethren, that flesh and blood cannot inherit the kingdom of God; neither doth corruption inherit incorruption. Behold, I shew you a mystery; We shall not all sleep, but we shall all be changed, in a moment, in the twinkling of an eye, at the last trump: for the trumpet shall sound, and the dead shall be raised incorruptible, and we shall be changed. For this corruptible must put on incorruption, and this mortal must put on immortality. So when this corruptible shall have put on incorruption, and this mortal shall have put on immortality, then shall be brought to pass the saying that is written, Death is swallowed up in victory. O death, where is thy sting? O grave, where is thy victory? The sting of death is sin; and the strength of sin is the law. But thanks be to God, which giveth us the victory through our Lord Jesus Christ. Therefore, my beloved brethren, be ye steadfast, unmoveable, always abounding in the work of the Lord, forasmuch as ye know that your labour is not in vain in the Lord.

I believe this with all my heart. I believe I will receive a new body, not subject to suffering and deterioration, whether it comes forth from the grave, or whether this old body I now have is still alive, and I am changed in a moment, at His return.

I don't know where some preachers and other Christian workers find the teaching that if one will only accept Christ, one's life will be a bed of roses from that moment onward. Most of us will still find our own particular thorns. Yes, our eyes will be opened with spiritual sight. Yes, our lives will take on new and worthwhile meaning. Yes, we will gain different values and priorities. These things will be true if we cultivate our faith. But we receive no guarantees that we will not suffer either for Christ or even by chance. One of the most meaningful aspects is that a personal faith in Christ can help us cope with suffering, loss of hope for recovery in this life, and fear. It is easier to trust Him in the dark if we walk with Him in the light.

It is said that the blood of the martyrs becomes the seed of the Church. The history of Christianity is a bloody one. From the crucifixion of Christ and the stoning of Stephen, the first martyr, to this present day, in some parts of the world, it is true. As I viewed the ruins of the ancient Colosseum in Rome, I wondered how many Christians had shed their life-blood on its floor to entertain Caesar and the Roman citizenry. As we were escorted through the catacombs, it seemed almost unbelievable that early Christians were forced to hide and make their homes in them. Christianity and the Caesars of Rome made a bloody period in history.

The struggle for Bible doctrine was a bloody one through the Dark Ages, as well as into the Reformation. Freedom of religion was the most noble motive for the settlement of our own nation. A careful review of American history, however, will reveal some shedding of blood over religious beliefs during our colonial period. While all this occurred, other people were fighting for their faith in other parts of the world. It causes one to wonder about one's own courage. I must bear the pain that has been given me until God says, "Enough!" But how brave would I be if pain was being inflicted upon me by others and I could stop it by agreeing to recant my faith? God helping me, I trust I would remain true. Yet it is something we might well think about more than once in a while.

Have you ever tried to imagine a world without pain? As mentioned, pain is a gift of God. It was no accident that it was built into God's creation of man and beast. It is both an alarm and a protective system. It immediately places us on guard when a part of our body suffers. Nothing gets one's attention like pain. It may be the sudden, accidental pain. It may be a pain demanding certain medications. It may be pain that demands we see a doctor, dentist, or someone else who can provide correct treatment. Often if we are injured, pain will prevent further compounding of that injury and demand the attention it needs. There is every possibility that it will call for the mobilization of the body's defense system to attack the cause of the pain. If I understand the objectives, many new medicines and treatments are being made to stimulate, or work with, the body's defense system to defeat the ravages of cancer and other undefeated diseases.

One of the tragedies of life is when one is born with a weak alarm and protective system. Another is when one contracts diseases that interfere with one's alarm system. Still another, one which we usually can avoid, is when one engages in activities that thwart the purpose of the system.

When I was a youth, boys who had done enough work to have callused hands liked to shock the girls by pushing pins through the calluses. Of course there was no pain unless we penetrated too deeply. There is a rare disease, with which a few are born, called congenital indifference to pain. It is possible for a small child to actually eat flesh from its fingers, hands, or other parts of its body and feel no pain. One can easily see what a curse such a disease would be.

There are diseases such as leprosy and diabetes that destroy the nerve endings. If unsupervised, a leper who had a foot involved in the disease might continue to drag the foot and completely wear it away. This could be true of any afflicted area in his body that was exposed to friction.

Alcohol and narcotics can anesthetize a person and prevent the registering of pain. One way we have of describing a person who is intoxicated is "He's feeling no pain." When I was a boy, one of the barbers in a neighboring town was known for his drinking and fast horses. One cold January Sunday his horses came back to town without him and with only part of his sporty buggy. When he was found, he was sitting in the middle of the frozen dirt road with a compound fracture of his left leg. The broken and protruding bones had even scraped some dirt and ice from the road. In his anesthe-tized condition, he was singing at the top of his voice and seemed to think the whole thing was amusing. It was not so humorous, however, when the leg had to be amputated. Over a few years he suffered more amputations and finally lost his life because of it. The failure to be able to suffer on the frozen road cost him dearly. I once asked one of my doctors if a nerve or two could not be severed and thus reduce, or relieve, my pain. He was quite adamant in his answer. He told me, if it were possible to do it, I would then strain my back without knowledge of it. Furthermore, I might even be able to walk on broken glass or tacks without feeling it. One surely can see, within reason, what a blessing pain is meant to be.

There are those who believe, at least to some extent, that God immediately punishes a person for a sin. This is like a small child being told not to touch the hot stove. He ignores the warning, disobediently touches the stove, and instanta-neously receives punishment. I agree that a small percent of punishments may happen so quickly. I also believe that some take years to happen, and some happen only after death. Let us open our eyes. The Psalmist and some of the Old Testa-ment prophets could not understand why some of the most sinful were also the richest, healthiest, and apparently the most blessed.

Can you imagine a world where all punishment came immediately, or even within a short time? People would be-come like trained animals. It would not be like the seal per-forming well to be rewarded with a fish, but it would be like the seal performing well to avoid punishment. What would happen to man's freedom? We would all be rushing to please, and our efforts would mean nothing more than self-preser-vation and freedom from pain. If our acts are to be truly virtuous and pleasing to God, we must know neither the pain nor the reward for doing them. The results must not be in evidence, proportionate to our merit, or little room will be

97

left for faith. It we truly trust God, we must trust Him when we don't understand what He is doing. Our God desires that we freely love Him, even in pain and misfortune. In fact, He would have His true followers cleave to Him when it appears they have every reason to turn away from Him or reject Him.

Suffering and pain are part of this world's experiences, and Christians are not exempt. During the last few years, tragedies of many kinds have befallen Christians and sinners alike. There have been calamities of nature—floods, hurricanes, mud slides, and earthquakes. War, terrorism, airplane crashes, world hunger, and homelessness strike unrelentingly the just and the unjust. Planet Earth reels in agony.

One cannot pastor long and not be called on to share many kinds of pain and suffering—his own and among his parishioners. The pain of job loss, the death of a loved one, or the birth of a handicapped child are to name but a few. Sometimes it seems Christians have more than their share, and we are tempted to self-pity, wounded pride, and a negative self-image. I have suffered each of these; but when I compare my life with others and realize how the Lord has blessed me, I can only feel fortunate in spite of my disability. Jesus came that we might have life and have it more abundantly. Certainly I have had the abundant life. What a privilege it is to lead people to Christ and then lead them in His Service. I have been privileged to travel around the world and in 48 of our 50 states. We have lived in some of the most beautiful spots on earth. These have left beautiful memories that will last through eternity.

Yes, Jesus died that we might have abundant and eternal life. He did not die to save us from suffering; He died to save us from hell. In addition, He showed us how to bear our suffering. There is no temptation known to man that Jesus did not experience. He was hungry, tired, and lonely. He was persecuted by mankind and assaulted by Satan. He voluntarily traded His heavenly glory for a body of bone, cartilage, sinew, flesh, and blood. A wonderful creation, the human body, but not to be compared with His glory. He suffered not only the pain, but also the shame, of the Cross. And He did it all for you and me.

Sometimes I play a little game with myself when feeling considerable pain, and ask myself what I would do if this was centuries ago. What if there was no pain medication? Or no anesthetic for certain tests and surgical procedures? Or no surgery, for that matter? How would I have survived? There are still places in this world where these things have not been developed, and we have not yet reached them with all our modern-day discoveries. Yes, indeed, things could be so much worse. It was only by the grace of God that we were born in the 20th century, as well as being born in America. It is also by His grace that we have been allowed to live through the most exciting and progressive period of history. Yes, things could be so much worse, regardless of what pain I must bear. I still have a road to travel, questions to be answered, and things to be seen before I will be satisfied.

At least for some, this would be a more satisfying story if God had completely healed me and, despite my age, placed me back into full-time service. Obviously this is not the case. This illness is not something that came upon me suddenly in the middle of my ministry, but it is something that has grown with me since birth. God has not chosen to stop it. But I rejoice in the years He has used me. I thank Him for the provisions He has made for my disability and retirement, when I did not have enough sense to make them myself. I have no desire to live through it all again, but neither do I have any regrets, nor would I want my life to have taken a different direction.

There are many things I do not understand in my own life and in the lives of others. It is good to be reminded, however, that where there seems to be an absence of meaning, there must be more faith. It's not necessary to know everything now. I can trust God, not only with my salvation, but in every way. He will do the right thing.

Some people have said, "I don't want God's justice; I want His mercy." We can understand this. Salvation would never have come to us if it depended upon His justice. Yet His justice is important. I have His mercy; I can depend upon His justice. To you who are discouraged with illness and pain, permit me to share my own conclusion. Don't waste too much time searching for the source and the reason. Simply know that if Jesus is your Savior, you certainly can trust God to do what is best. Even in times of greatest depression, you can know that He who made and controls the universe cares for you. He is our God! With Job we can say, "Though he slay me, yet will I trust in him" (13:15).